CRITIQUE OF
PRACTICAL REASON

Third Edition

The Library of Liberal Arts

OSKAR PIEST, FOUNDER

. . . .

IMMANUEL KANT

Critique of
Practical Reason

Edited and translated, with notes
and introductions by

LEWIS WHITE BECK

THIRD EDITION

The Library of Liberal Arts

. . . .

published by

PRENTICE HALL, Upper Saddle River, New Jersey 07458

LIBRARY OF CONGRESS CATALOGING-IN-PUBLICATION DATA
Kant, Immanuel, 1724-1804.
 [Kritik der praktischen Vernunft. English]
 Critique of practical reason / Immanuel Kant; edited and translated,
with notes and introductions, by Lewis White Beck.—
3rd ed.
 p. cm.—(The Library of liberal arts)
Includes bibliographical references (p.   ).
ISBN 0-02-307753-0 (paper)
 1. Ethics. I. Beck, Lewis White. II. Title. III. Series:
Library of liberal arts (Macmillan Publishing Company)
B2773.E5B4   1993
170—dc20   92-17421
                                                 CIP

Editor: Maggie Barbieri
Production Supervisor: Bert Yaeger
Production Manager: Muriel Underwood
This book was set in Garamond Light by Digitype, Inc.

Prentice
Hall ©1993 by Prentice-Hall, Inc.
      Upper Saddle River, New Jersey 07458

Printed in the United States of America
      17 18 19 20

ISBN   0-02-307753-0

Prentice-Hall International (UK) Limited, London
Prentice-Hall of Australia Pty. Limited, Sydney
Prentice-Hall of Canada Inc., Toronto
Prentice-Hall Hispanoamericana, S.A., Mexico
Prentice-Hall of India Private Limited, New Delhi
Prentice-Hall of Japan, Inc., Tokyo
Prentice-Hall Asia Pte. Ltd., Singapore
Editora Prentice-Hall do Brasil, Ltda., Rio de Janeiro

CONTENTS

CRITIQUE OF PRACTICAL REASON

TRANSLATOR'S INTRODUCTION

I

Immanuel Kant's *Critique of Practical Reason*, published in 1788, is the second of his three *Critiques*, the others being the *Critique of Pure Reason* (1781) and the *Critique of the Faculty of Judgment* (1790). It is likewise the second of his three most important writings in moral philosophy, the first being the *Foundations of the Metaphysics of Morals* (1785), and the third being the *Metaphysics of Morals* (1797).

The relation between the *Critique of Practical Reason* and the *Foundations of the Metaphysics of Morals* is much like that between the *Critique of Pure Reason* and the *Prolegomena*. For each of the first two *Critiques*, Kant wrote a briefer, less "scholastic," work on the same topics. The shorter works follow the analytical or regressive method; they begin with experience and regress upon its a priori presuppositions or principles without which it would not be possible to have that kind of experience. In these shorter works, starting points are found in mathematical and scientific knowledge (*Prolegomena*) and in "common knowledge of morality" (in the *Foundations*). In each, everything is based "upon something already known as trustworthy, from which we can set out with confidence and ascend to sources as yet unknown."[1] These "sources as yet unknown" are the forms of intuition and categories (in the *Prolegomena*) and the moral law and freedom (in the *Foundations*).

The method of the *Critiques*, on the other hand, is synthetic. That is, they begin with principles and thence proceed to experiences which they organize, conceptualize, and render intelligible. Only by this method can philosophical knowledge "present all its articulations, as the structure of a peculiar cog-

[1] *Prolegomena* §4.

nitive faculty, in their natural combination."[2] The *Critique of Practical Reason*, therefore, begins as it were where the *Foundations* ends, and retraces its steps. For this reason, Kant tells us, the *Critique of Practical Reason* presupposes the *Foundations* only "in so far as that work gives a preliminary acquaintance with the principle of duty and justifies a definite formula of it; otherwise it is an independent work."[3] This definite formula, of course, is the categorical imperative, reached in the second section of the *Foundations* and in §7 of the *Critique*.

To be more specific, the *Foundations*, as the work giving an analysis of ordinary moral consciousness, begins with ordinary moral judgments and the felt constraint of duty. It seeks to bring their basis to light, and does so by formulating the moral law expressed as a categorical imperative and a theory of freedom as the condition for making and realizing the demands of this imperative. The *Critique of Practical Reason*, on the other hand, begins with definitions, and proceeds quickly, in a quasi-deductive manner, to the formula of the moral law and the theory of freedom. The works, therefore, for a considerable distance go along the same path, but in opposite directions.

Nevertheless, the *Critique* contains material which, Kant says, would be out of place in the *Foundations*, for it must show the unity of practical and theoretical reason. The full investigation of this unity constitutes the chief advance made in the *Critique of Practical Reason* beyond Kant's earlier work. This unity was asserted in the first *Critique* and assumed in the *Foundations*: only in the *Critique of Practical Reason* is this assumption "deduced" or justified. Only in the light of this larger and deeper problem of showing that there is no conflict of reason with itself in its claims to knowledge and in its use in practical conduct does Kant deal adequately with many of those most profound philosophical problems concerning the relations among knowing, believing, and acting.

[2]Ibid., Introduction (Macmillan ed., p. 11).
[3]*Critique of Practical Reason*, this edition, p. 8.

II

Even the titles of the works, properly understood, tell much of this story of their intimate connection. There is a whole theory implicit in the very words "metaphysics of morals," "critique," and "practical reason."

"Metaphysics" means two things for Kant. It is presumed speculative knowledge of supersensible and unconditional reality; this is the old metaphysics which the *Critique of Pure Reason* was written to destroy. Then there is the metaphysics Kant attempted to establish, "metaphysics as science," "the inventory of all our possessions through pure reason, systematically arranged,"[4] "a system of a priori knowledge from mere concepts."[5] It has two parts: the metaphysics of nature, consisting of all the a priori principles of our knowledge of what is, and the metaphysics of morals, comprising all the a priori principles of what ought to be.[6] But many philosophers claimed that certain, rational knowledge of God, freedom, and immortality belonged in the storehouse of metaphysics understood as knowledge of ultimate reality. Kant is primarily concerned to deny this, and he does so by showing that such putative knowledge has no valid foundation. Claims to such knowledge are vain and empty or, in Kant's technical terminology, "dialectical."

This brings us to Kant's conception of the function he assigns to "critique." One task of critique is the self-examination of reason for the purpose of discovering and eradicating the dialectical illusions of the older metaphysics. The second task of critique is to rescue those principles that constitute metaphysics "as science" from the ruin threatened by universal empiricism, which not only raised doubts about the possibility of speculative metaphysics but also tended to undermine knowledge even of nature and morals.[7] Critique is negatively an at-

[4] *Critique of Pure Reason*, A xx.

[5] *Metaphysics of Morals*, Introduction, ii.

[6] *Critique of Pure Reason*, A 840 = B 868.

[7] *Critique of Practical Reason*, this edition, p. 12 and the ironical remark at the end of the Preface, p. 14.

tack on pretensions to supersensible knowledge, which appear as metaphysical dogmatism and moral fanaticism;[8] affirmatively it establishes the structure, range, use, and validity of concepts (like that of cause in the first *Critique*, duty in the second) that cannot be objectively valid if derived from experience, but that are essential if science and morals are to "make sense." Without critique having both these affirmative and negative functions, Kant thinks it is not possible to draw a line between legitimate and illegitimate metaphysics, or to defend legitimate knowledge from attacks properly made only on dialectical illusion masquerading as higher wisdom.

So much for the word "critique." And what is "practical reason"? To say, as Kant does, that practical reason is the same as will is instructive only when we understand his theory of reason itself. In the *Critique of Pure Reason* there are three cognitive faculties of the mind: sensibility, which is receptivity to sensations under the forms of space and time; understanding, which is the faculty of conceptualizing and synthesizing data into knowledge of objects, the synthesis occurring under rules established by concepts called categories; and reason, which is the faculty of synthesizing knowledge of objects into systems (such as the "realm of nature," the whole system of phenomena under laws). Reason guides the construction of knowledge in its systematic aspect, by directing our search for the absolute conditions of all contingent conditions, which will support the entire edifice of knowledge. This is the ideal of reason in its theoretical aspect; but when its search leads it to make assertions that concern supersensible realities that belong in the realm of the older metaphysics, it produces only philosophical illusions.

Now, Kant tells us, all things in nature, including human beings, behave in accordance with laws. But only a rational being can have and act according to a *conception* of laws. A falling body, for instance, "obeys" Galileo's law in the sense of merely illustrating it; but human beings endowed with con-

[8]Ibid., pp. 88, 143.

sciousness and reason, can govern their behavior by their *conception* of this law. By their knowledge of Galileo's law, they may decide whether it is safe to jump from a certain height, and may thereby overcome their fear of doing so. Such a conception of law is possible only for a rational being; and we say that a man or woman acts voluntarily when his or her conception of a law, and not a momentary impulse, governs his or her behavior. To take another example: a man as a creature of impulse unwittingly instantiates psychological "laws" in sexual behavior; but as a rational being, possessing insight into the causal laws of psychology, he may discern consequences of his possible actions, and thereby modify his behavior and act in ways which in fact thwart his impulses. Such a man, we ordinarily say, has a strong will; he acts rationally, not merely impulsively; rational order and system are introduced into his activities by the governance of reason.

We can thus see that when Kant says the will is nothing but practical reason, what he says is not so very startling, but is implicit even in the common usage of the word "will." "Will" is the name we ordinarily give to the subjective experience of control of impulse by reason, and not to the merely emotional or impulsive aspect of behavior.

The book before us is a critical examination of will understood in this sense, as practical reason, *reason applied in conduct*. And its main thesis is that though practical reason generally has an impulsive component or drive, which it more or less successfully guides by maxims and rules of experience, it is also possible for one's reason to guide one's behavior without any drive springing from variable, subjective impulses directed to the gaining of pleasure. Such reason provides not just long-range control of impulses but, as *pure* practical reason, it can provide the motives and even set the goals of action. The law conceived by reason in this capacity is not an empirical law of nature, not even a law of human nature learned from psychology—no, it is moral law, and the imperative to obey it is a categorical imperative, not hypothetical and contingent upon the actual presence of a given impulse.

Kant tells us, in the opening sentence, that the work is called *Critique of Practical Reason* and not *Critique of Pure Practical Reason* because its task is to show that pure reason can be practical, and it does so by a critical examination of reason's *entire* (both pure and empirical) practical use. This suggests that this *Critique* has only the second, the affirmative, function distinguished above. But this is not correct, for there is a dialectical illusion even in pure practical reason, as we shall see; and this must be resolved. — The lack of parallelism in the titles is unfortunate in another respect: it has led superficial readers and a not insignificant number of philosophical thinkers into believing that Kant established a dichotomy between "pure" and "practical" reason. But if this is believed, it is safe to say that not a single doctrine of his ethical theory has been or can be understood. Kant is trying to show that pure reason can be practical, and must be practical if morality is not an illusion; he is trying to show that it is practical of itself, and not merely as "the slave of the passions" (Hume), or other, nonrational components of personality.[9]

We are now in a position to appreciate the full import of the title of the book, *Critique of Practical Reason*. Affirmatively, the book is to work out the pure a priori laws of conduct, and thus to establish beyond doubt that pure reason can be practical and that the principles of pure reason will constitute a metaphysics of morals understood as rational knowledge of the moral law in all its ramifications. Negatively, it will examine the presuppositions of practical reason to prevent them from being passed off as insight into a supersensible world. These two tasks are carried out, respectively, in the Analytic of Pure Practical Reason and in the Dialectic of Pure Practical Reason.

III

The Analytic has as its task the establishment of the possibility of a priori (universal and necessary) practical principles

---

[9]As held by Aristotle (*Nicomachaean Ethics*, 1139a, 1177b; *On the Soul*, 432b) and most other philosophers and psychologists.

(moral laws), and it accomplishes this in the first two chapters. They give the formula of the moral law (§ 7), its differences from maxims and rules of practice (§§ 1–4), its intimate relation to the autonomy (freedom) of the will as practical reason (§§ 5, 6, 8, and pp. 43–51), and the connection between moral principles and moral concepts (good and evil) (Chapter II). Chapter III of the Analytic is one of the most effective of all of Kant's writings, manifesting on every page his own profound moral commitment and giving a vivid and memorable phenomenology of moral experience. Its purpose is to show the way in which human beings come to be moved by the thought of duty; and this account of reverence for the law as the motive to morality has important implications for Kant's theory of moral education, as given in the Methodology at the end of this *Critique*.

Though the argument is somewhat more formal, elaborate, and rigorous, most of the Analytic will be at least partly familiar to those who have read the *Foundations*, and I shall therefore turn to new material not touched upon, or at most intimated, in the *Foundations* but fully developed in the present work. Most of this material is in the Dialectic.

IV

To understand fully the Dialectic of the second *Critique*, we must recall some of the teachings of the *Critique of Pure Reason*.[10] In the Dialectic of that book, Kant was concerned with claims that the human mind inevitably makes (when not forewarned by critical philosophy) — to have knowledge of what is beyond the sphere of possible sense experience. The mind claims to have knowledge from pure reason unrestricted by the

---

[10]Fortunately, at various places in the second *Critique*, Kant reminds the reader of what he has said in the first. But inasmuch as these passages may appear somewhat cryptic to anyone who has not read the first *Critique*, it is perhaps permissible also for me to try to give a brief summary of this part of his theory of knowledge.

conditions of our senses; such knowledge of the intelligible world is claimed to exist in speculative metaphysics. Now speculative metaphysics, however unwarranted its assertions, is not idle twaddle; reason makes claims to such knowledge not arbitrarily, but for a perfectly sound purpose: as rational beings, who want to know the "reasons" for things, we seek for completeness in knowledge, with no unsupported foundations and no loose ends. Such completeness is not achievable by simply adding empirical facts and more empirical facts to the infinitely expandable store of factual information. Not more knowledge, but a different kind of knowledge, is required if our knowledge is to be seen as a coherent, perfect, and self-supporting whole. No sane man has ever claimed to possess such a perfect omniscience; but some more or less vague ideal of what such knowledge would be like has been effective in the history of science and philosophy from Parmenides to Einstein. What Kant does in the Dialectic of the first *Critique* is to show that this ideal inevitably leads to certain specific metaphysical dogmas. Such systematic organization of our knowledge, he says, would have to include knowledge that there are first causes in the world, that there are permanent substances, and that there is a necessary being. These are the familiar doctrines of classical rationalistic metaphysics: that the will is free, the soul immortal, and God real.

Yet any theoretical argument to show that these are true is dialectical, i.e., fallacious and illusory. The Dialectic of pure theoretical reason is the exposure of the fallacies involved in all such arguments. Kant does not thereby prove that these metaphysical dogmas are false; he merely shows that they cannot be known to be true on grounds of theoretical knowledge, and that reason's speculative need for such truths is bound to go unsatisfied and frustrated — that, in the end, "it embraces not Juno, but a cloud."

Minor details aside, much of Kant's argument as well as his conclusions would be acceptable to many philosophers of today who base their skepticism of metaphysics on quite other considerations; this aspect of Kant's philosophy makes him one of the most important antecedents of pragmatism and modern positivism. But then Kant goes further, and attempts to show not merely the unattainability of this kind of ideal knowledge but also its undesirability. *If* such knowledge of supersensible reality *were* possible, it would be found to be in conflict with the conceptual foundations of morality.

In the preface to the second edition of the *Critique of Pure Reason*, which was written while the *Critique of Practical Reason* was taking shape in Kant's mind, he wrote: "I have found it necessary to deny *knowledge* [of supersensible reality] in order to make room for *faith*. The dogmatism of metaphysics [i.e., the belief that there is knowledge of God, freedom, and immortality] is the source of all that unbelief, always very dogmatic, which wars against morality,"[11] the dogmatism of metaphysics being simply an extension of the principles of empirical nature (which principles exclude freedom, God, and immortality) to supersensible reality. But by denying knowledge, he necessarily leaves a "vacant place" at the apex of our pursuit of knowledge.[12] In its negative function, the *Critique of Pure Reason* clips the wings of speculation to keep it from presumptuously trying to fill this (cognitively) empty place with its own unproved Ideas.

We are now ready to examine the Dialectic of the second *Critique*. Assume, for the moment, that morality entails belief in God, freedom, and immortality — why Kant says it does so will be mentioned later. If reason in its practical aspect (as the "organ" of morality) requires that the theoretically empty space in the system of knowledge be filled by assumptions, in default of which the moral experience would be illusory and the moral law invalid; and if these assumptions conflict with no principles that theoretical reason can *establish*; then, says Kant, pure reason in its practical capacity has primacy over pure reason in its speculative (theoretical) capacity. It can therefore legitimately make — indeed, for the sake of morality it must

[11]*Critique of Pure Reason*, B xxx.
[12]*Critique of Practical Reason*, pp. 50, 108.

make — these assumptions. But it makes them not as claims of knowledge but as matters of faith, or as what Kant calls "practical postulates."[13] If we mistook the authority of practical reason and claimed that these postulates gave us any knowledge, we would not only exceed the competence of theoretical reason but would actually threaten the foundations of morals themselves.[14]

The ideas of God, freedom, and immortality are merely possible for speculative reason, not actual. But Kant says that they are necessary for morality. They therefore fit this "empty space" in the system of theoretical knowledge, and acceptance of them is justified by the primacy of practical reason.

We turn now to the final question: how does Kant show that morality requires such postulates? The same answer does not fit all of them. The postulate of freedom differs markedly from the others, and therefore we must briefly discuss each of them separately. Generally speaking, we can say that freedom is required for the establishment of the moral law itself, while the other postulates are required only for the resolution of an antinomy into which practical reason itself falls.

In the Dialectic of the *Critique of Pure Reason*, Kant de-

---

[13] *Critique of Practical Reason*, Bk. II, ch. II, sect. 3: "On the Primacy of Pure Practical Reason in its Association with Speculative Reason." This chapter should be carefully compared with the writings of other defenders of the "right" or "will" to believe beyond theoretical evidence, among whom Kant is often counted. But the differences between Kant and, for instance, William James and Kierkegaard are at least as important as the similarities. The chief difference is, in Kantian language, that since they have not shown that pure reason can be practical (which, indeed, they deny), their claim that there is a right to believe beyond the evidence is based on premises having no objective validity, and the resulting belief is therefore irrational and subjective. Kant, on the other hand, claims that the legitimate belief in these postulates is objective and rational, though not cognitive; it is based on demands of pure reason and not on what James called "our passional nature." What is unique in Kant's view is precisely the point that "rational" is not restricted in meaning to "cognitive." See Kant's reply to Thomas Wizenmann, p. 151.

[14] *Critique of Practical Reason*, Bk. II, ch. II, sect. 9: "Of the Wise Adaptation of Man's Cognitive Faculties to his Practical Vocation."

velops an antinomy between the concept of freedom and that of natural causation. That is, he gives a proof that the connection of events under the laws of nature is the only necessary connection, and then he gives an equally valid proof that there is a "causality of freedom," i.e., that new causal chains can occur in nature. The first member of such a chain might be an act of will which is not an effect of some earlier natural event. He resolves this antinomy by arguing that both statements are true and that there is no contradiction between them. The first is true, but it concerns events only as phenomena in time. If the empirical events that are the objects of scientific knowledge were events among things in themselves, the principle of natural causation would be absolutely true without restriction, there would be an irresolvable conflict between freedom and causal determinism, and freedom would have to be surrendered. But if the events we observe are only phenomena, i.e., appearances of things in themselves as organized by our own sensibility and understanding, as he believes he has shown, in others parts of the *Critique of Pure Reason*, to be the case, then the causality of freedom might hold of the relation of realities to appearances while mechanical determinism would still hold of the connections among the observed events themselves. The two principles might therefore be true, each in its own context. Thus the *Critique of Pure Reason* shows that freedom is not incompatible with natural necessity and is thus a possible concept. But the first *Critique* does not have the task of showing that it is actual, i.e., that there *is* freedom.[15]

The *Critique of Practical Reason*, however, shows that the moral law, which is given as a "fact of pure reason," reciprocally implies and is implied by the concept of freedom.[16] In as-

---

[15]This is not quite true in fact, for there are sections of the *Critique of Pure Reason* that are concerned with moral questions. It would be more accurate to say: a critique restricted to an examination of theoretical and speculative reason would give no grounds for asserting more than the possibility of the Idea of freedom.

[16]*Critique of Practical Reason*, pp. 4, 28f., 31.

serting that human beings are morally obligated, Kant is asserting that freedom is real, even though nature, including human
nature, can be understood *scientifically* only under the principle of strict causal necessity. Kant's concept of freedom is not
equivalent to that according to which free actions have no
causes, or to the theory (soft determinism), popular in his time
and in ours, that actions are free if they are psychologically determined by one's own settled character and not by momentary
stimuli.[17] Kant holds the more daring conception that there is a
causality of freedom, or a noumenal and a phenomenal causation; in present-day terminology he holds a theory of *real
agency* and compatibilism.[18]

The other two postulates are quite different, and it is generally recognized, even by Kant himself, that the argument for
them is less coercive. Pure practical reason has its own antinomy and the exposure and resolution of this antinomy is the
negative task of the *Critique of Practical Reason*. It arises in the
concept of "the highest good," which is the ideal of moral perfection conjoined with happiness proportionate to the degree
of perfection attained. Striving for the highest good is required
by the moral law, but the highest good cannot be made real unless the soul is immortal and God exists. The moral law is vain if
it commands us to do the impossible; hence either the moral
law is invalid, or the highest good is possible. Now since we
have the "fact of pure reason"[19] to show that the moral law
really does bind us, and since the criticism of speculative reason showed no impossibility in either immortality or God (but
only the impossibility of a theoretical proof of them), the assumptions are justified. They are held by rational faith, and not
in the form of a claim to metaphysical knowledge of the nature
of ourselves and of the being of God.

Hence the *Critique of Practical Reason* performs two func-

[17]Ibid, pp. 97ff.
[18]See Allen W. Wood, "Kant's Compatibilism," in *Self and Nature in Kant's
Philosophy* (Cornell University Press, 1984).
[19]*Critique of Practical Reason*, pp. 31, 43.

tions: affirmatively it defends those concepts without which moral experience would be unintelligible or impossible; negatively it restrains dogmatism and fanaticism that claim on moral grounds to have an insight into ultimate metaphysical realities.

There is a tale, invented by Heinrich Heine, that Kant demolished religious belief, but when he saw how unhappy this made his servant Lampe, the great philosopher showed that he was also a kindly man by writing the *Critique of Practical Reason* to give old Lampe his faith again. This is, of course, a caricature of the doctrine of the primacy of practical reason and its postulates. But if readers will keep this story in mind as they read the Dialectic, so that at the end they can decide whether there is a kernel of truth inside the husk of error in this anecdote, they can rightly feel that they have at least the beginning of real insight into what is perhaps the most important and profound philosophy of morals produced in modern times.

SKETCH OF KANT'S LIFE AND WORK

Immanuel Kant was born in Königsberg, East Prussia, (now Kaliningrad, Russia) April 22, 1724. His family were among the Pietists, a Protestant sect somewhat like the Quakers and early Methodists. Pietism's deeply ethical orientation and singular lack of emphasis on theological dogmatism became a part of Kant's nature and a determining factor in his philosophy. After attending the University of Königsberg and serving as tutor in several aristocratic families, Kant became an instructor at the university. He held this position for fifteen years, lecturing and writing on metaphysics, logic, ethics, and the natural sciences. In the sciences he made significant but, at the time, little recognized contributions, especially in physics, astronomy, geology, and meteorology.

In 1770 he was appointed Professor of Logic and Metaphysics at Königsberg, and in 1781 he published his most important work, the *Critique of Pure Reason*. This work opened up new fields of study and problems for him at an age when most men are ready to retire; but for Kant there followed a period of nearly twenty years of unremitting labor and unparalleled accomplishment. Merely a list of the most important writings shows this: *Prolegomena to Any Future Metaphysics* (1783); *Idea for a Universal History* (1784); *Foundations of the Metaphysics of Morals* (1785); *Metaphysical Foundations of Natural Science* (1786); second edition of *Critique of Pure Reason* (1787); *Critique of Practical Reason* (1788); *Critique of the Faculty of Judgment* (1790); *Religion within the Limits of Reason Alone* (1793); *Perpetual Peace* (1795); *Metaphysics of Ethics* (1797); *Anthropology from a Pragmatic Point of View* (1798); *The Conflict of the Faculties* (1798). He died in Königsberg, February 12, 1804.

Kant's personality, or at least a caricature of it, is well known. Most people who know nothing else of Kant do know that the

CRITIQUE OF PRACTICAL REASON

housewives of Königsberg used to set their clocks by the regular afternoon walk he took, and that his life was said to pass like the most regular of regular verbs. But a truer picture of his personality — less pedantic, Prussian, and Puritanical — comes to us from the German writer Johann Gottfried Herder:

> I have had the good fortune to know a philosopher. He was my teacher. In his prime he had the happy sprightliness of a youth; he continued to have it, I believe, even as a very old man. His broad forehead, built for thinking, was the seat of an imperturbable cheerfulness and joy. Speech, the richest in thought, flowed from his lips. Playfulness, wit, and humor were at his command. His lectures were the most entertaining talks. His mind, which examined Leibniz, Wolff, Baumgarten, Crusius, and Hume, and investigated the laws of nature of Newton, Kepler, and the physicists, comprehended equally the newest works of Rousseau . . . and the latest discoveries in science. He weighed them all, and always came back to the unbiased knowledge of nature and to the moral worth of man. The history of men and peoples, natural history and science, mathematics and observation, were the sources from which he enlivened his lectures and conversation. He was indifferent to nothing worth knowing. No cabal, no sect, no prejudice, no desire for fame could ever tempt him in the slightest away from broadening and illuminating the truth. He incited and gently forced others to think for themselves; despotism was foreign to his mind. This man, whom I name with the greatest gratitude and respect, was Immanuel Kant.

NOTE ON THE REVISED EDITION

The first edition of this translation was published by the University of Chicago Press in 1949. It underwent minor emendations in subsequent printings by the Liberal Arts Press and by Macmillan, but the present edition is substantially revised.

The underlying text is that of the Royal Prussian Academy of Sciences (Berlin, 1912), edited by Paul Natorp. Intentional departures from that edition are indicated in brackets and footnotes. The marginal pagination and the pagination in the running heads refer to the Academy edition. Kant's prodigal use of *Fettdruck* and *Sperrdruck* has not been followed in our sparing use of italics.

I am grateful to reviewers of earlier editions and other Kant scholars (especially Dr. Robert J. Benton) for detecting some errors which I am now glad to correct.

GLOSSARY

Kant often gives formal definitions of his terms, but then disregards them. It is unfeasible to insist on translating a word in German always by the same word in English. But I wish to call attention to several lexical decisions I have had to make.

1. *Vorstellung*, the generic name for any content of consciousness, is translated as "representation" when verbal exactitude in a technical expression is called for; in less formal contexts it is translated as "conception," "thought," or "idea."

2. *Idee*, referring to a concept of reason to which no intuition is adequate, is translated as "Idea" (capital *I*). When used less formally and technically, it is translated as "idea" (lower case *i*).

3. *Sinnlich* and its derivatives are translated as "sensible," and so on, in epistemological and metaphysical contexts. They are translated as "sensuous," and so forth, when they refer to emotions and sentiments.

4. *Wille* and *Willkür* are translated as "will" and "choice," respectively.

5. *Triebfeder* is translated as "drive" (Abbott's "spring," and, in earlier Beck editions, "incentive").

6. *Bestimmungsgrund des Willens* is translated sometimes as "ground of determination of the will" and sometimes as "motive."

7. *Allgemeine Gesetzgebung*, following Paton, is translated sometimes as "giving universal law" instead of "universal legislation."

8. *Achtung* is translated as "respect," "reverence" being reserved for *Ehrfurcht*.

9. *Ding an sich* is an expression Kant employs only once in the second *Critique*, his usual locution being *Ding an sich selbst*. According to Gerold Prauss (*Kant und das Problem der Dinge an sich* [Bonn, 1974]) the latter locution is adverbial rather than adjectival, and elliptical for "thing regarded as it is in itself." The distinction is important, because the first suggests that there are two *kinds* of things, viz., appearances and things in themselves, whereas the second suggests that there is one kind of thing in two contexts (as it appears, and as it is regarded in itself). The locution "thing in itself" is so deeply entrenched in philosophical writing that I do not wish to challenge it in the medium of a translation and a footnote, though I have argued elsewhere for a "two-aspect" rather than a "two-thing" interpretation. I use the longer expression where I think the shorter and less cumbersome form is likely to be misleading.

10. *Absicht* translated as "intention."

BIBLIOGRAPHY

ABBOTT, THOMAS KINGSMILL, trans. *Kant's Critique of Practical Reason and Other Works on the Theory of Ethics, with a Memoir of Kant.* London: Longmans Green, 1873 (sixth edition, 1909).

FERRY, LUC, AND HEINZ WISMANN, trans. *Critique de la raison pratique,* in *Kant. Oeuvres philosophiques,* vol. 2, pp. 609–804. Paris: Gallimard, 1985. (Contains instructive notes.)

* * *

ALLISON, HENRY E. *Kant's Theory of Freedom.* Cambridge: Cambridge University Press, 1990.

AMERIKS, KARL. *Kant's Theory of Mind.* Oxford: Clarendon Press, 1982.

BECK, LEWIS WHITE. *A Commentary on Kant's Critique of Practical Reason.* Chicago: University of Chicago Press, 1960. German translation, *Kant's "Kritk der praktischen Vernunft,"* by Karl-Heinz Ilting. Munich: Wilhelm Fink Verlag, 1974.

BENTON, ROBERT J. *Kant's Second Critique and the Problem of Transcendental Arguments.* The Hague: Nijhoff, 1977.

BITTNER, RÜDIGER, AND KONRAD CRAMER, EDS. *Materialien zu Kants Kritik der praktischen Vernunft.* Frankfurt: Suhrkamp, 1975.

CAIRD, EDWARD. *The Critical Philosophy of Immanuel Kant,* vol. 2. Glasgow: Maclehose, 1889.

CARNOIS, BERNARD. *The Coherence of Kant's Doctrine of Freedom,* trans. by David Booth. Chicago: University of Chicago Press, 1987.

KRONER, RICHARD. *Kant's Weltanschauung,* trans. by John E. Smith. Chicago: University of Chicago Press, 1956.

PATON, H. J. *In Defence of Reason.* London: Hutchinson, 1951.

——. *The Categorical Imperative.* Chicago: University of Chicago Press, 1948.

SULLIVAN, ROGER W. *Immanuel Kant's Moral Theory.* Cambridge: Cambridge University Press, 1989.

WOOD, ALLEN W. *Kant's Moral Religion*. Ithaca: Cornell University Press, 1970.

ZELDIN, MARY-BARBARA. *Freedom and the Critical Undertaking: Essays on Kant's Later Critiques*. Ann Arbor: University Microfilms International, 1980.

CRITIQUE OF
PRACTICAL REASON

PREFACE

Why this *Critique* is called simply *Critique of Practical* [3]
Reason and not *Critique of Pure Practical Reason*, though the
parallelism between it and the critique of speculative reason
seems to demand the latter title, will be sufficiently shown in
the treatise itself. Its task is merely to show that there is a pure
practical reason, and, in order to do this, it critically examines
reason's entire practical faculty. If it succeeds in this task, there
is no need to examine the pure faculty itself to see whether it,
like speculative reason, presumptuously overreaches itself.
For if pure reason is actually practical, it will show its reality and
that of its concepts in action, and all disputations which aim to
prove its impossibility will be in vain.

With the pure practical faculty of reason, the reality of transcendental freedom is also confirmed. Indeed, it is substan-
tiated in the absolute sense needed by speculative reason in its
use of the concept of causality, for this freedom is required if
reason is to rescue itself from the antinomy in which it is inevitably entangled when attempting to think the unconditioned in
a causal series. For speculative reason, the concept of freedom
was problematic but not impossible; that is to say, speculative
reason could think of freedom without contradiction, but it
could not assure any objective reality to it. Reason showed
freedom to be conceivable only in order that its supposed impossibility might not endanger reason's very being and plunge
it into an abyss of skepticism.

The concept of freedom, in so far as its reality is proved by an
apodictic law of practical reason, is the keystone of the whole
architecture of the system of pure reason and even of speculative reason. All other concepts (those of God and immor- [4]
tality) which, as mere Ideas, are unsupported by anything in
speculative reason now attach themselves to the concept of
freedom and gain, with it and through it, stability and objective

[4]

3

reality. That is, their *possibility* is proved by the fact that there really is freedom, for this Idea is revealed by the moral law.

Freedom, however, among all the Ideas of speculative reason is the only one whose possibility we know a priori. We do not understand it, but we know it as the condition* of the moral law which we do know. The Ideas of God and immortality are, on the contrary, not conditions of the moral law, but only conditions of the necessary object of a will which is determined by this law, this will being merely the practical use of our pure reason. Hence we cannot say that we *know* or *understand* either the reality or even the possibility of these Ideas. Nevertheless, they are conditions of applying the morally determined will to the object (the highest good) which is given to it a priori. Consequently, the possibility of these conditions can and *must* be assumed in this practical context without our knowing or understanding them in a theoretical sense. To serve their practical function, it suffices that they not contain any internal impossibility (contradiction). Here we have a ground of assent which, in contrast to speculative reason, is only subjective, but which is just as objectively valid to an equally pure but practical reason. Thus, through the concept of freedom, the Ideas of God and immortality gain objective reality and legitimacy and indeed subjective necessity (as a need of pure reason). Reason is not thereby extended, however, in its theoretical [5] knowledge; the only thing which is different is that the possibility, which was heretofore a problem, now becomes an assertion, and the practical use of reason is thus connected with the elements of theoretical reason. This need is not just a hypothet-

---

*To avoid having anyone imagine that there is an inconsistency when I say that freedom is the condition of the moral law and later assert that the moral law is the only condition under which freedom can be known, I will only remind the reader that, though freedom is certainly the *ratio essendi* of the moral law, the latter is the *ratio cognoscendi* of freedom. For had not the moral law already been distinctly thought in our reason, we would never have been justified in assuming anything like freedom, even though it is not self-contradictory. But if there were no freedom, the moral law would never have been encountered in us.

ical one for some *arbitrary* speculative purpose, of the kind that one must assume if he *wishes* to complete the use of reason in speculation; it is rather a need, *with the status of a law*, to assume that without which an aim cannot be achieved which one *ought* to set before himself invariably in all his actions.

It would certainly be more satisfying to our speculative reason if those problems could be solved just by themselves without such a detour and if insight into them could be put up for practical use; but our speculative faculty is not so conveniently disposed. Those who boast of such elevated knowledge should not hold it back but present it for public testing and acclaim. They wish to *prove*; very well, let them prove, and the critical philosophy will lay down its weapons before them as victors. *Quid statis? Nolint. Atqui licet esse beatis.*[1] Since they do not actually wish to prove, presumably because they cannot, we must again take up these weapons and seek, in the practical use of reason, sufficient grounds for the concepts of God, freedom, and immortality. These concepts are founded upon the moral use of reason, while speculation could not find sufficient guarantee even of their possibility.

Now is explained the enigma of the critical philosophy, which lies in the fact that we must renounce the objective reality of the supersensible use of the categories in speculation and yet can attribute this reality to them in respect to the objects of pure practical reason. This must have seemed an inconsistency so long as the practical use of reason was known only by name. However, a thorough analysis of the practical use of reason makes it clear that the reality thought of here implies no theoretical determination of the categories and no extension of our knowledge to the supersensible. One then perceives that all that is meant in attributing reality to those concepts is that an object is attributable to them either in so far as they are contained in the necessary determination of the will a priori or be-

[1]An allusion to Horace *Satire* I, 1, 19. A god gives men the privilege of changing places with each other. The god speaks: "What are you waiting for? Maybe they don't wish to change, yet they might be happy."

cause they are indissolubly connected with the object of this determination. The inconsistency vanishes because the use which is now made of these concepts is different from [6] that required by speculative reason.

So far from being incoherent, the highly consistent structure of the *Critique of Pure Reason* is very satisfyingly revealed here. For in that work the objects of experience as such, including even our own subject, were explained as only *appearances*, though as based upon things regarded as they are in themselves; consequently, even in that *Critique* it was emphasized that the supersensible was not mere fancy and that its concepts were not empty. Now practical reason itself, without any collusion with the speculative, provides reality to a supersensible object of the category of causality, i.e., to freedom. This is a practical concept and as such is subject only to practical use; but what in the speculative critique could only be thought is now confirmed by fact. The strange but incontrovertible assertion of the speculative *Critique*, that the thinking subject is only an appearance to itself in inner intuition, now finds its full confirmation in the *Critique of Practical Reason*; the establishment of this thesis is here so cogent that one would be compelled to accept it even if the first had not already proved it.*

In this way I can also understand why the most weighty criticisms of the *Critique* which have come to my attention turn about these two points: first, the reality of the categories as applied to noumena, which is denied in theoretical knowledge but affirmed in practical; and, second, the paradoxical demand to regard one's self, as subject to freedom, as noumenon, and yet from the point of view of nature to think of one's self as a phenomenon in one's own empirical consciousness. So long as

---

*The union of causality as freedom with causality as the mechanism of nature, the first being given through the moral law and the latter through natural law, and both as related to the same subject, man, is impossible unless man is conceived by pure consciousness as a being in itself in relation to the former, but by empirical reason as appearance in relation to the latter. Otherwise the self-contradiction of reason is unavoidable.

one had no definite concept of morality and freedom, no conjecture could be made concerning what the noumenon was which should be posited as the ground of the alleged appearance, and even whether it was possible to form a concept of it, since all the concepts of the pure understanding in their theoretical employment had already been assigned exclusively to mere appearances. Only a detailed *Critique of Practical Reason* can set aside all these misconceptions and put in a [7] clear light the consistency which constitutes its chief merit.

So much for the justification of the fact that the concepts and principles of the pure speculative reason are now and again reexamined in this work, in spite of the fact that they have already been scrutinized in the *Critique of Pure Reason*. This might not seem proper in the systematic construction of a science, since matters which have already been decided should only be referred to and not discussed again. But here it is allowed and even necessary, for these concepts of reason are now seen in transition to an altogether different use from that made of them in the first *Critique*. Such a transition makes necessary a comparison of their old and new employment, in order to distinguish clearly the new path from the previous one and at the same time to call attention to the connection between them. One must not, therefore, think that such considerations, including those devoted to the concept of freedom in the practical use of pure reason, are only interpolations which serve to fill out gaps in the critical system of speculative reason, for this is complete in its design. They are not like the props and buttresses which usually have to be put behind a hastily erected building, but they are rather true members making the structure of the system plain and letting the concepts, which were previously thought of only in a problematic way, be clearly seen as real.

This reminder pre-eminently concerns the concept of freedom, for it is surprising that so many boast of being able to understand it and to explain its possibility, yet see it only psychologically. But if they had carefully pondered it from a transcendental standpoint, they would have seen its indispensability as a problematic concept in the complete use of speculative reason as well as its complete incomprehensibility; and if they subsequently passed over to the practical use of this concept, they would have been brought to the same description of it in respect to its principles which they are now so unwilling to acknowledge. The concept of freedom is the stumbling block of all empiricists but the key to the most sublime practical principles for critical moralists, who see, through it, that they must necessarily proceed rationally. For this rea- [8] son, I beg the reader not to run lightly through what is said about this concept at the end of the Analytic.

I leave it to the connoisseur of this kind of work to judge whether such a system into which practical reason has been developed through a critique of this faculty has cost much or little trouble, especially in gaining the right point of view from which the whole can be rightly sketched. It presupposes the *Foundations of the Metaphysics of Morals*, but only in so far as that work gives a preliminary acquaintance with the principle of duty and justifies a definite formula of it*; otherwise it is an independent work.

The reason the classification of all practical sciences is not completely carried through, as the *Critique of Speculative Reason* did this for the theoretical sciences, lies in the nature of the practical faculty of pure reason itself. For the specific definition of duties as human duties, which is necessary to a classification of them, is possible only if the subject of this definition

---

*A critic^a who wished to say something against that work really did better than he intended when he said that there was no new principle of morality in it but only a new formula. Who would want to introduce a new principle of morality and, as it were, be its inventor, as if the world had hitherto been ignorant of what duty is or had been thoroughly wrong about it? Those who know what a formula means to a mathematician, in determining what is to be done in solving a problem without letting him go astray, will not regard a formula which will do this for all duties as something insignificant and unnecessary.

^{a}Gottlob August Tittel, who in his *Über Herrn Kants Moralreform* (1786), asked, "Is the entire Kantian reform of ethics to limit itself just to a new formula?"

(man) is known in his actual nature, at least in so far as this knowledge is needed in determining his relation to duty in general. Getting this knowledge, however, does not belong in a critique of practical reason as such, which gives an account of the principles of the possibility of duty, of its extent and limits, without particular reference to human nature. Consequently, this classification belongs to the system of science, not to the system of criticism.

I have, I hope, given a sufficient answer, in the second part of the Analytic, to a certain critic,[2] truth-loving and acute and therefore worthy of respect, who made the following objection to the *Foundations of the Metaphysics of Morals:* the concept of the good was not established before the moral principle, [9] as in his opinion was necessary.* I have also paid attention to many other objections which have come to me from men who show that the discovery of truth lies close to their hearts, and I shall continue to do so; but those who have their old system so much before their eyes that they have already decided what should be approved or disapproved desire no discussion [10] which could stand in the way of their private views.

---

[2]The anonymous author (H. A. Pistorius) of a review of the *Foundations* in *Allgemeine deutsche Bibliothek*, LXVI, Part 2, 447 ff. See Daniel Jentsch's letter to Kant, May 14, 1787.

*One could also raise the objection that I have not previously explained the concept of the faculty of desire or the feeling of pleasure. This reproach would be unfair, however, because this explanation, as given in psychology, could reasonably be presupposed. But then the definition given in psychology might be so framed that the feeling of pleasure would be made basic to the determination of the faculty of desire (as this is commonly done); and, as a result, the supreme principle of practical philosophy would necessarily turn out to be empirical, a conclusion which would have to be proved first and which is, in fact, completely refuted in this *Critique*. Therefore, I shall give this explanation in the way it ought to be given in order to decide properly this controversial question at the beginning.

Life is the faculty of a being by which it acts according to the laws of the faculty of desire. The *faculty of desire* is the faculty such a being has of causing, through its ideas, the reality of the objects of these ideas. *Pleasure* is the idea of the agreement of an object or an action with the *subjective* conditions of life,

When it is a question of determining the origin, contents, and limits of a particular faculty of the human mind, the nature of human knowledge makes it impossible to do otherwise than begin with an exact and (as far as is allowed by the knowledge[3] we have already gained) complete delineation of its parts. But still another thing must be attended to which is of a more philosophical and architectonic character. It is to grasp correctly the idea of the whole, and then to see all those parts in their reciprocal interrelations, in the light of their derivation from the concept of the whole, and as united in a pure rational faculty. This examination and the attainment of such a view are obtainable only through a most intimate acquaintance with the system. Those who are loath to engage in the first of these inquiries and who do not consider acquiring this acquaintance worth the trouble will not reach the second stage, the synoptic view, which is a synthetic return to that which was previously given only analytically. It is not to be wondered at if they find inconsistencies everywhere, though the gaps which they presume to find are not in the system itself but in their own incoherent train of thought.

---

i.e., with the faculty through which an idea causes the reality of its object (or the direction of the energies of a subject to such an action as will produce the object).

I need no more than this for the purposes of a critique of concepts borrowed from psychology; the rest is supplied by the *Critique* itself. The question as to whether pleasure is always the ground of the faculty of desire or whether under certain conditions it only follows upon a particular modification of this faculty —this question, as is easily seen, remains unanswered by this explanation; for it consists only of terms belonging to the pure understanding, i.e., categories, which contain nothing empirical. Such a precaution against making judgments by venturing definitions before a complete analysis of concepts has been made (usually only far along in a system) is to be recommended throughout philosophy, but it is often neglected. It will be noticed throughout the critiques of both the theoretical and the practical reason that there are many opportunities for supplying inadequacies and correcting errors in the old dogmatic procedure of philosophy which were detected only when concepts, used according to reason, were seen in reference to the whole of reason.

[3]Reading *Erkenntnis* with Vorländer instead of *Elemente*.

I have no fear, with respect to this treatise, of the reproach that I wish to introduce a new language, since the kind of thinking it deals with is very close to the popular way of thinking. This objection, moreover, could not have been made even to the first *Critique* by anyone who had really thought his way through it instead of merely turning the pages. To make up new words for accepted concepts when the language does not lack expressions for them is a childish effort to distinguish one's self not by new and true thoughts but by new patches on old clothes. If any reader of that work can show that he knows more common expressions which are as adequate to the thoughts as the ones I used seemed to me, or can demonstrate the nullity of the thoughts themselves and therewith of the terms used to express them, he should do so. The first would greatly oblige me, for I only want to be understood; the second would be a service to philosophy itself. But, as long as those thoughts stand, [11] I very much doubt that expressions both more suitable to them and more common can be found.*

In this manner the a priori principles of two faculties [12] of the mind, cognition and desire, are to be discovered and their scope and limits determined. Thus the firm basis is laid for a systematic philosophy, both theoretical and practical, as a science.

---

* More than this kind of unintelligibility, I fear some misinterpretations, here and there, of expressions which I have sought out with the greatest care in order that the concepts which they mean may not be missed. Thus, under the heading "modality," in the table of categories of practical reason, the "permitted" and the "forbidden" (objective-practical meanings of the possible and the impossible) have almost the same significance, in popular usage, as the categories which immediately follow them, namely, "duty" and "contrary to duty." Here, however, the former mean that which is in agreement or disagreement with a merely *possible* precept (as, for example, the solution of problems of geometry or mechanics); the latter, however, indicate what is in such a relation to a law actually lying in reason as such. This difference of meaning is not entirely foreign to ordinary language, but it is somewhat unusual. For instance, an orator is not permitted to forge new words or constructions, but this is permitted, to some extent, to a poet. In neither case, though, is there any thought of duty, for if anyone wishes to forfeit his reputation as a speaker, no one can prevent him. Here it is a question of the difference of the imperatives correspond-

Nothing worse could happen to all these labors, however, than that someone[4] should make the unexpected discovery that there is and can be no a priori knowledge at all. But there is no danger of this. It would be like proving by reason that there is no such thing as reason; or we say that we know something through reason only when we know that we could have known it even if it had not actually come within our experience. Thus knowledge through reason and a priori knowledge are the same thing. It is a clear contradiction to try to extract necessity from an empirical proposition (*ex pumice aquam*),[5] and it is equally contradictory to attempt to procure, along with such necessity, true universality to a judgment (for without it no rational inference is possible, and consequently no inference is possible by analogy either, since the latter has an at least pre-

ing to the problematic, assertoric, and apodictic ground of determination. Similarly in the note where I compare the moral ideals of practical perfection in the various philosophical schools, I have differentiated between the Ideas of wisdom and holiness, although I have shown them to be fundamentally and objectively identical. But I take wisdom, in that note, only in the sense in which man (the Stoic, for example) lays claim to it, and thus as it is thought of subjectively as a human characteristic. (Perhaps the term "virtue," which the Stoic made so much of, would show even better the characteristic of this school.) But the term "postulate of pure practical reason" can occasion the worst misinterpretation if confused with the meaning which postulates have in pure mathematics, where they are of apodictic certainty. The latter, however, postulate the possibility of an action, the object of which one previously knows a priori, theoretically and with complete certainty, to be possible. Those of the pure practical reason, however, postulate the possibility of an object (God and the immortality of the soul) from apodictic practical laws, but therefore only for the use of a practical reason. This certainty of the postulated possibility is not in the least theoretical and consequently also not apodictic, i.e., not a necessity known by the reference to an object; it is a necessary assumption, rather, with reference to the subject as conforming to the objective practical laws of reason. Thus it is merely a necessary hypothesis. I could not discover for this subjective yet true and absolute rational necessity a better term than "postulate."

[4]The rather acerbic tone from here to the end of the Preface is directed against J. G. Feder, the author of *Über Raum und Caussalität*[sic] *zur Prüfung der kantischen Philosophie* (1787) and editor of the notorious review of the first *Critique*, which led to the polemics of the *Prolegomena*.

[5]"Water from a pumice stone" (Plautus *Persa* i. i. 14).

sumed universality and objective necessity and therefore presupposes it). To substitute subjective necessity, i.e., custom,
for the objective which pertains only to a priori judgments
would be to deny to reason the faculty of judging an object, of
knowing it and what belongs to it. It would mean, for example,
that what usually or always follows a certain prior condition
could not be inferred to follow *from* it, since that would imply
objective necessity and an a priori concept of a connection. It
would mean only that similar cases may be expected, as animals expect them. It would be to reject the concept of cause as
fundamentally false and a mere delusion of thought. As to attempting to remedy this lack of objective and consequently
universal validity by arguing that one sees no reason not to attribute to other reasonable beings a different type of ideation —
well, if this sort of argument should yield a valid inference,
then our ignorance would render us greater services in widen-
ing our knowledge than all our reflections. Simply because we
do not know any reasonable beings other than men, we would
have the right only to assume them to be of the same nature as
we know ourselves to be, and therefore we would really know
them. I need not mention the fact that universality of assent
does not prove the objective validity of a judgment, i.e., [13]
its validity as knowledge, but only call attention to the fact that,
even if sometimes that which is universally assented to is also
correct, this is no proof of its agreement with the object; it is
rather the case that only objective validity affords the ground of
a necessary universal agreement.

Hume would find himself completely at ease in this system
of universal empiricism of principles, for he desired, as is well
known, nothing more than that a merely subjectively necessary
concept of cause, i.e., custom, be assumed in place of all objective meaning of necessity in the causal concept; he did this in
order to deny to reason any judgment concerning God, freedom, and immortality; and he knew very well how to draw conclusions with complete cogency when once the principles
were conceded. But even Hume did not make his empiricism
so universal as to include mathematics in it. He held its propo-

sitions to be analytic, and, if this were correct, they would indeed be apodictic; but this would not give us any right to conclude that there is a faculty of reason which can make apodictic judgments also in philosophy, for in philosophy they would be synthetic, as the law of causality is. But if one assumes a universal empiricism, mathematics will also be involved.

When, however, mathematics comes into conflict with that reason which admits only empirical principles, as this inevitably occurs in the antinomy, since mathematics irrefutably proves the infinite divisibility of space which empiricism cannot allow, there is an obvious contradiction between the highest possible demonstrable evidence and presumed inferences from empirical principles. One might ask, like Cheselden's[6] blind man, "Which deceives me, sight or touch?" (Empiricism is based on touch, but rationalism on a necessity into which we can have insight.) Thus universal empiricism is revealed to be genuine skepticism, which has been falsely ascribed to Hume in this unlimited sense,* for he let mathematics stand as a sure touchstone of experience, instead of admitting no touch- [14] stone (which can be found only in a priori principles) even though experience consists not merely of feelings but also of judgments.

Since in this philosophical and critical age no one can be very much in earnest about such an empiricism, and since it is presumably put forward only as an exercise for judgment and to place the necessity of rational principles in a clearer light by contrast, we can only be grateful to those who trouble themselves with this otherwise uninstructive work.

[6]William Cheselden (1688–1752), an English surgeon, famous for his operation of iridectomy which cured some forms of blindness.

*Names which refer to the followers of a sect have always been accompanied by much injustice. It is as if someone said, "N. is an idealist." For although he not only admits, but even emphasizes, that our ideas of external things correspond to real objects, he will still hold that the form of their intuition depends not on them but on the human mind.

INTRODUCTION

OF THE IDEA OF A *CRITIQUE OF PRACTICAL REASON*

The theoretical use of reason is concerned with objects [15] of the merely cognitive faculty, and a critical examination of it with reference to this use deals really only with the pure cognitive faculty, because the latter raised the suspicion, which was subsequently confirmed, that it might easily pass beyond its boundaries and lose itself among unattainable objects or even among contradictory concepts. It is quite different with the practical use of reason. In the latter, reason deals with the grounds determining the will, which is a faculty either of bringing forth objects corresponding to conceptions or of determining itself, i.e., its causality to effect such objects (whether the physical power is sufficient to this or not). For here reason can at least attain so far as to determine the will, and, in so far as it is a question of volition only, reason does always have objective reality.

This, then, is the first question: Is pure reason sufficient of itself to determine the will, or is it only as empirically conditioned that it can do so? At this point there appears a concept of causality which is justified by the *Critique of Pure Reason,* though subject to no empirical exhibition. That is the concept of freedom, and if we now can discover means to show that freedom does in fact belong to the human will (and thus to the will of all rational beings), then it will have been proved not only that pure reason can be practical but also that it alone, and not the empirically conditioned reason, is unconditionally practical. Consequently, we shall have to make a critical examination, not of the *pure* practical reason, but only of prac- [16] tical reason *as such.*

For pure [practical] reason, once it is demonstrated to exist, is in no need of a critical examination; it is pure reason itself which contains the standard for the critical investigation of its entire use. The critique, therefore, of practical reason as such has the obligation to prevent the empirically conditioned reason from presuming to be the only ground of determination of the will. The use of pure [practical] reason, if it is shown that there is such a reason, is alone immanent; the empirically conditioned use of reason, which presumes to be sovereign, is, on the contrary, transcendent, expressing itself in demands and commands which go far beyond its own sphere. This is precisely the opposite situation from that of pure reason in its speculative use.

Yet because it is still pure reason, the knowledge of which here underlies its practical use, the organization of the *Critique of Practical Reason* must conform, in its general outline, to that of the *Critique of Speculative Reason*. We shall therefore have to have a Doctrine of Elements and a Methodology. The former must have as its first part an Analytic as the rule of truth and a Dialectic as an exhibition and resolution of illusion in the judgments of practical reason, only the order in the subdivision of the Analytic will be the reverse of that in the *Critique of Speculative Reason*. For in the present work we begin with principles and proceed to concepts, and only then, if possible, go on to the senses, while in the study of speculative reason we had to start with the senses and end with principles. Again the reason for this lies in the fact that here we have to deal with a will and to consider reason not in relation to objects but in relation to this will and its causality. The principles of the empirically unconditioned causality must come first, and afterward the attempt can be made to establish our concepts of the ground of determination of such a will, their application to objects, and finally their application to the subject and its sensuous faculty. The law of causality from freedom, i.e., any pure practical principle, is the unavoidable beginning and determines the objects to which it alone can be applied.

PART I
DOCTRINE OF THE ELEMENTS OF PURE PRACTICAL REASON

BOOK I
ANALYTIC OF PURE PRACTICAL REASON

CHAPTER I
PRINCIPLES OF PURE PRACTICAL REASON

§1. *Definition*

Practical principles are propositions which contain a [19] general determination of the will, having under it several practical rules. They are subjective, or maxims, when the condition is regarded by the subject as valid only for his own will. They are objective, or practical laws, when the condition is recognized as objective, i.e., as valid for the will of every rational being.

REMARK

Assuming that *pure* reason can contain a practical ground sufficient to determine the will, then there are practical laws. Otherwise all practical principles are mere maxims. In the will of a rational being affected by feeling, there can be a conflict of maxims with the practical laws recognized by this being. For example, someone can take as his maximum not to tolerate any unavenged offense and yet see at the same time that this is only his own maxim and not a practical law and that, if it is taken as a rule for the will of every rational being, it would be inconsistent with itself.

In natural science the principles of what occurs (e.g., the

principle of equivalence of action and reaction in the communication of motion) are at the same time laws of nature, for there the use of reason is theoretical and determined by [20] the nature of the object. In practical philosophy, which has to do only with the grounds of determination of the will, the principles which a man makes for himself are not laws by which he is inexorably bound, because reason, in practice, has to do with a subject and especially with his faculty of desire, the special character of which may occasion variety in the rule. The practical rule is always a product of reason, because it prescribes action as a means to an effect which is its purpose. This rule, however, is an imperative for a being whose reason is not the sole determinant of the will. It is a rule characterized by an "ought," which expresses the objective necessitation of the act and indicates that, if reason completely determined the will, the action would without exception take place according to the rule.

Imperatives, therefore, are valid objectively and are quite distinct from maxims, which are subjective principles. Imperatives determine either the conditions of causality of a rational being as an efficient cause only in respect to its effect and its sufficiency to bring this effect about, or they determine only the will, whether it be adequate to the effect or not. In the former case, imperatives would be hypothetical and would contain only precepts of skill; in the latter, on the contrary, they would be categorical and would alone be practical laws. Maxims are thus indeed principles, but they are not imperatives. Imperatives themselves, however, when they are conditional, i.e., when they determine the will not as such but only in respect to a desired effect, are hypothetical imperatives, which are practical precepts but not laws. Laws must completely determine the will as will, even before I ask whether I am capable of achieving a desired effect or what should be done to realize it. They must thus be categorical; otherwise they would not be laws, for they would lack the necessity which, in order to be practical, must be completely independent of pathological conditions [see footnote, p. 78—Trans.], i.e., conditions only contingently related to the will.

Tell someone, for instance, that in his youth he should work and save in order not to want in his old age — that is a correct and important practical precept of the will. One easily sees, however, that the will is thereby directed to something else which he is assumed to desire; and, as to this desire, we must leave it up to the man himself if he foresees other resources than his own acquisitions, does not even hope to reach old age, or thinks that in case of need he can make do with little. Reason, from which alone a rule involving necessity can be derived, gives necessity to this precept, without which it would not be an imperative; but this necessity is dependent on only subjective conditions, and one cannot assume it in equal measure in all men. But for reason to give law it is required that reason need presuppose only itself, because the rule is objectively [21] and universally valid only when it holds without any contingent subjective conditions which differentiate one rational being from another.

Now tell a man that he should never make a deceitful promise; this is a rule which concerns only his will regardless of whether any purposes he has can be achieved by it or not. Only the volition is to be completely determined a priori by this rule. If, now, it is found that this rule is practically right, it is a law, because it is a categorical imperative. Thus practical laws refer only to the will, irrespective of what is attained by its causality, and one can disregard this causality (as belonging to the sensuous world) in order to have the laws in their purity.

§2. *Theorem I*

All practical principles which presuppose an object (material) of the faculty of desire as the determining ground of the will are without exception empirical and can hand down no practical laws.

By the term "material of the faculty of desire," I understand an object whose reality is desired. When the desire for this object precedes the practical rule and is the condition under which the latter becomes a principle, I say, first, that this principle is then always empirical. I say this because the determining ground of choice consists in the conception of an object and its relation to the subject, whereby the faculty of desire is determined to seek its realization. Such a relation to the subject is called pleasure in the reality of an object, and it must be presupposed as the condition of the possibility of the determination of choice. But we cannot know, a priori, from the idea of any object, whatever the nature of this idea, whether it will be associated with pleasure or displeasure or will be merely indifferent. Thus any such determining ground of choice must always be empirical, and the practical material principle which has it as a condition is likewise empirical.

Second, a principle which is based only on the subjective susceptibility to a pleasure or displeasure (which is never known except empirically and cannot be valid in the same form for all rational beings) cannot function as a law even to the subject possessing this susceptibility, because it lacks [22] objective necessity, which must be known a priori. For this reason, such a principle can never furnish a practical law. It can, however, be counted as a maxim of a subject thus susceptible.

§3. *Theorem II*
All material practical principles are, as such, of one and the same kind and belong under the general principle of self-love or one's own happiness.

Pleasure from the representation of the existence of a thing, in so far as it is a determining ground of the desire for this thing, is based upon the susceptibility of the subject because it depends upon the actual existence of an object. Thus it belongs to sense (feeling) and not to the understanding, which expresses a relation of a representation to an object by concepts and not the relation of a representation to the subject by feelings. It is practical only in so far as the faculty of desire is determined by the sensation of agreeableness which the subject expects from the actual existence of the object. Now happiness is a rational being's consciousness of the agreeableness of life which without interruption accompanies his whole existence, and to make this the supreme ground for the determination of choice constitutes the principle of self-love. Thus all material principles, which place the determining ground of choice in the pleasure or displeasure to be received from the reality of any object whatsoever, are entirely of one kind. Without exception they belong under the principle of self-love or one's own happiness.

COROLLARY

All material practical rules place the ground of the determination of the will in the lower faculty of desire, and if there were no purely formal laws of the will adequate to determine it, we could not admit [the existence of] any higher faculty of desire.

REMARK I

It is astonishing how otherwise acute men believe they can find a difference between the lower and the higher faculty of desire by noting whether the representations which are [23] associated with pleasure have their origin in the senses or in the understanding. When one inquires into the determining grounds of desire and finds them in an expected agreeableness resulting from something or other, it is not a question of where the representation of this enjoyable object comes from, but merely of how much the object can be enjoyed. If a representation, even though it has its origin and status in the understanding, can determine choice only by presupposing a feeling of pleasure in the subject, then its becoming a determining ground of choice is wholly dependent on the nature of the inner sense, i.e., it depends on whether the latter can be agreeably affected by that representation. However dissimilar the representations of the objects, be they proper to understanding or even the reason instead of to the senses, the feeling of pleasure, by virtue of which they constitute the determining ground of the will (since it is the agreeableness and enjoyment which one expects from the object which impels the activity toward producing it) is always the same. This sameness lies not merely in the fact that all feelings of pleasure can be known only empirically, but even more in the fact that the feeling of pleasure always affects one and the same life-force which is manifested in the faculty of desire, and in this respect one determining ground can differ from any other only in degree. Otherwise how could one make a comparison with respect to magnitude between two determining grounds the ideas of which depend upon different faculties, in order to prefer the one which affects the faculty of desire to the greater extent? A man can return unread an instructive book which he cannot again obtain, in order not to miss the hunt; he can go away in the middle of a fine speech, in order not to be late for a meal; he can leave an intellectual conversation, which he otherwise enjoys, in order to take his place at the gambling table; he can even repulse a poor man whom it is usually a joy to aid, because he has only enough money in his pocket for a ticket to the theater. If the determination of the will rests on the feelings of agreeableness or disagreeableness which he expects from any cause, it is all the same to him through what kind of representation he is affected. The only thing he considers in making a choice is how great, how long-lasting, how easily obtained, and how often repeated this agreeableness is. As the man who wants money to spend does not care whether the gold in it was mined in the mountains or washed from the sand, provided it is accepted everywhere as having the same value, so also no man asks, when he is concerned only with the agreeableness of life, whether the representations are from sense or understanding; he asks only how much and how great is the pleasure which they will afford him over the longest time.

Only those who would like to deny to pure reason the power of determining the will without presupposing any feeling whatsoever could deviate so far from their own exposition [24] as to describe as quite heterogeneous what they have previously brought under one and the same principle. Thus, for instance, a person can find satisfaction in the mere exercise of power, in the consciousness of spiritual strength in overcoming obstacles in the way of his designs, and in the cultivation of intellectual talents. We correctly call these the more refined joys and delights, because they are more in our power than others and do not wear out, but, rather, increase our capacity for even more of this kind of enjoyment; they delight and at the same time cultivate. But this is no reason to pass off such pleasures as a mode of determining the will different from that of the senses. For the possibility of these [refined] pleasures, too, presupposes, as the first condition of our delight, the existence in us of a corresponding feeling. So to assume this difference resembles the error of ignorant persons who wish to dabble in metaphysics and who imagine matter as so subtle, so supersubtle, that they almost get dizzy considering it, and then believe that they have conceived of a spiritual but still extended being. If, with Epicurus, we let virtue determine the will only because of the pleasure it promises, we cannot later blame him for holding that this pleasure is of the same sort as those of the coarsest senses. For we have no reason to charge him with relegating the representations by which this feeling is excited in us to the bodily senses only. So far as we can tell, he sought the source of many of them in the employment of the higher cognitive faculty. In accordance with the principles stated above, that did not and could not deter him, however, from holding that the pleasure which is given to us by these intellectual representations and which is the only means by which they can determine the will is of exactly the same kind as that coming from the senses.

Consistency is the highest obligation of a philosopher and yet the most rarely found. The ancient Greek schools afford more examples of it than we find in our syncretistic age, when a certain shallow and dishonest system of coalition between contradictory principles is devised because it is more acceptable to a public which is satisfied to know a little about everything and at bottom nothing, thus playing the jack-of-all-trades. The principle of one's own happiness, however much reason and understanding may be used in it, contains no other determinants for the will than those which belong to the lower faculty of desire. Either, then, no higher faculty of desire exists, or else pure reason alone must of itself be practical, i.e., it must be able to determine the will by the mere form of the practical rule without presupposing any feeling or consequently any representation of the pleasant or the unpleasant as the matter of the faculty of desire and as the empirical condition of its principles. Then only is reason a truly higher faculty of desire, but still only in so far as it determines the will by itself and not in the service [25] of the inclinations. Subordinate to reason as the higher faculty of desire is the pathologically determinable faculty of desire, the latter being really and in kind different from the former, so that even the slightest admixture of its impulses impairs the strength and superiority of reason, just as taking anything empirical as the condition of a mathematical demonstration would degrade and destroy its force and value. Reason determines the will in a practical law directly, not through an intervening feeling of pleasure or displeasure, even if this pleasure is taken in the law itself. Only because, as pure reason, it can be practical is it possible for it to give law.

REMARK II

To be happy is necessarily the desire of every rational but finite being, and thus it is an unavoidable determinant of its faculty of desire. Contentment with our existence is not, as it were, an inborn possession or bliss, which would presuppose a consciousness of our self-sufficiency; it is rather a problem imposed upon us by our own finite nature as a being of needs. These needs are directed to the material of the faculty of desire, i.e., to that which is related to a basic subjective feeling of pleasure or displeasure, determining what we require in order to be satisfied with our condition. But just because this material ground of determination [motive] can be known by the subject only empirically, it is impossible to regard this demand for happiness as a law, since the latter must contain exactly the same determining ground for the will of all rational beings and in all cases. Since, though, the concept of happiness always underlies the practical relation of objects to the faculty of desire, it is merely the general name for subjective grounds of determination [motives], and it determines nothing specific concerning what is to be done in a given practical problem; but in a practical problem this is what is alone important, for without some specific determination the problem cannot be solved. Where one places one's happiness is a question of the particular feeling of pleasure or displeasure in each person, and even of the differences in needs occasioned by changes of feeling in one and the same person. Thus a subjectively necessary law (as a law of nature) is objectively a very contingent practical principle which can and must be very different in different people. It therefore cannot yield any [practical] law, because in the desire for happiness it is not the form (accordance with law) but only the material which is decisive; it is a question only of whether I may expect pleasure from obedience to this law, and, if so, how much. Principles of self-love can indeed contain universal rules of skill (how to find means to some end), but [26] these are only theoretical principles* as, for example, how someone who wants bread should construct a mill. But practical precepts based on them can never be universal, for what determines the faculty of desire is based on the feeling of pleasure and displeasure, which can never be assumed to be directed to the same objects by all people.

But suppose that finite rational beings were unanimous in the kind of objects their feelings of pleasure and pain had, and even in the means of obtaining the former and preventing the latter. Even then they could not set up the principle of self-love as a practical law, for the unanimity itself would be merely contingent. The determining ground would still be only subjectively valid and empirical, and it would not have the necessity which is conceived in every law, an objective necessity arising from a priori grounds, unless we hold this necessity to be not at all practical but only physical, maintaining that our action is as

---

*Propositions called "practical" in mathematics or natural science should properly be called "technical," for in these fields it is not a question of determining the will; they only indicate the manifold of a possible action which is adequate to bring about a certain effect, and are therefore just as theoretical as any proposition which asserts a connection between cause and effect. Whoever chooses the latter must also choose the former.

inevitably forced upon us by our inclination as yawning is by seeing others yawn. It would be better to maintain that there are no practical laws but merely counsels for the service of our desires than to elevate merely subjective principles to the rank of practical laws, which must have an objective and not just subjective necessity and which must be known a priori by reason instead of by experience, no matter how empirically universal. Even the rules of uniform phenomena are denominated natural laws (for example, mechanical laws) only if we really can understand them a priori or at least (as in the case of those of chemistry) suppose that they could be known in this way if our insight went deeper. Only in the case of subjective practical principles is it expressly made a condition that not objective but subjective conditions of choice must underlie them, and hence that they must be represented always as mere maxims and never as practical laws.

This remark may appear at first blush to be mere hairsplitting; actually, it defines the most important distinction which can be considered in practical investigations.

§4. *Theorem III*

If a rational being can think of his maxims as practical [27] universal laws, he can do so only by considering them as principles which contain the determining grounds of the will because of their form and not because of their matter.

The material of a practical principle is the object of the will. This object either is the determining ground of the will or it is not. If it is, the rule of the will is subject to an empirical condition (to the relation of the determining representation to feelings of pleasure or displeasure), and therefore the rule is not a practical law. If all material of a law, i.e., every object of the will considered as a ground of its determination, is taken from it, nothing remains except the mere form of giving universal law. Therefore, a rational being either cannot think of his subjectively practical principles (maxims) as at the same time universal laws, or he must suppose that their mere form, through which they are fitted for being given as *universal* laws, is alone that which makes them a practical law.

REMARK

What form in a maxim fits it for universal law-giving and what form does not do so can be distinguished without instruction by the most common understanding. I have, for example, made it my maxim to augment my property by every safe means. Now I have in my possession a deposit, the owner of which has died without leaving any record of it. Naturally, this case falls under my maxim. Now I want to know whether this maxim can hold as a universal practical law. I apply it, therefore, to the present case and ask if this maxim could take the form of a law, and consequently whether I could, by the maxim, make the law that every man is allowed to deny that a deposit has been made when no one can prove the contrary. I immediately realize that taking such a principle as a law would annihilate itself, because its result would be that no one would make a deposit. A practical law which I acknowledge as such must qualify for being universal law; this is an identical and therefore a self-evident proposition. Now, if I say that my will is subject to a practical law, I cannot put forward my inclination (in this case, my avarice) as fit to be a determining ground of a universal practical law. It is so far from being worthy of giving universal laws [28] that in the form of universal law it must destroy itself.

It is therefore astonishing how intelligent men have thought of proclaiming as a universal practical law the desire for happiness, and therewith to make this desire the determining ground of the will merely because this desire is universal. Though elsewhere natural laws make everything harmonious, if one here attributed the universality of law to this maxim, there would be the extreme opposite of harmony, the most arrant conflict, and the complete annihilation of the maxim itself and its purpose. For the wills of all do not have one and the same object, but each person has his own (his own welfare), which, to be sure, can accidentally agree with the purposes of others who are pursuing their own, though this agreement is far from sufficing for a law because the occasional exceptions which one is permitted to make are endless and cannot be definitely comprehended in a universal rule. In this way a harmony may result resembling that depicted in a certain satirical poem

as existing between a married couple bent on going to ruin,
"Oh, marvelous harmony, what he wants is what she wants"; or
like the pledge which is said to have been given by Francis I to
the Emperor Charles V, "What my brother wants (Milan), that I
want too." Empirical grounds of decision are not fit for any external legislation, and they are just as little suited to an internal,
for each man makes his own subject the foundation of his inclination, and in each person it is now one and now another inclination which has preponderance. To discover a law which
would govern them all by bringing them into unison is absolutely impossible.

§5. *Problem I*

Granted that the mere legislative form of maxims is the sole
sufficient determining ground of a will, find the character of
the will which is determinable by it alone.

Since the mere form of a law can be thought only by reason
and is consequently not an object of the senses and therefore
does not belong among appearances, the conception of this
form as the determining ground of the will is distinct from all
determining grounds of events in nature according to the law
of causality, for these grounds must themselves be appearances. Now, as no determining ground of the will except [29]
the universal legislative form [of its maxim] can serve as a law
for it, such a will must be conceived as wholly independent of
the natural law of appearances in their mutual relations, i.e., the
law of causality. Such independence is called *freedom* in the
strictest, i.e., transcendental, sense. Therefore, a will to which
only the law-giving form of the maxim can serve as a law is a
free will.

§6. *Problem II*

Granted that a will is free, find the law which alone is competent to determine it necessarily.

Since the material of the practical law, i.e., an object of the
maxim, cannot be given except empirically, and since a free
will must be independent of all empirical conditions (i.e.,

those belonging to the world of sense) and yet be determinable, a free will must find its ground of determination in the law, but independently of the material of the law. But besides the latter there is nothing in a law except the legislative form. Therefore, the legislative form, in so far as it is contained in the maxim, is the only thing which can constitute a determining ground of the [free] will.

REMARK

Thus freedom and unconditional practical law reciprocally imply each other. I do not here ask whether they are actually different, instead of an unconditional law being merely the self-consciousness of pure practical reason, and thus identical with the positive concept of freedom.[1] The question now is whether our *knowledge* of the unconditionally practical takes its inception from freedom or from the practical law. It cannot start from freedom, for this we can neither know immediately, since our first concept of it is negative, nor infer from experience, since experience reveals only the law of appearances and consequently the mechanism of nature, the direct opposite of freedom. It is therefore the moral law, of which we become immediately conscious as soon as we construct maxims for the will, which first presents itself to us; and, since reason [30] exhibits it as a ground of determination which is completely independent of and not to be outweighed by any sensuous condition, it is the moral law which leads directly to the concept of freedom.

But how is the consciousness of that moral law possible? We can come to know pure practical laws in the same way we know pure theoretical principles, by attending to the necessity with which reason prescribes them to us and to the elimination from them of all empirical conditions, which reason directs. The concept of a pure will arises from the former, as the consciousness of a pure understanding from the latter. That this is the correct organization of our concepts, and that morality first re-

[1]Reading *dieses*, with Paton, instead of *diese*.

veals the concept of freedom to us while practical reason deeply perplexes the speculative with this concept which poses the most insoluble of problems, is shown by the following considerations. First, nothing in appearances is explained by the concept of freedom, but there the mechanism of nature must be the only clue. Second, there is the antinomy of pure reason which arises when reason aspires to the unconditioned in a causal series and which involves it in inconceivabilities on both sides, since at least mechanism has a use in the explanation of appearances, while no one would dare introduce freedom into science had not the moral law and, with it, practical reason come and forced this concept upon us.

Experience also confirms this order of concepts in us. Suppose that someone says his lust is irresistible when the desired object and opportunity are present. Ask him whether he would not control his passion if, in front of the house where he has this opportunity, a gallows were erected on which he would be hanged immediately after gratifying his lust. We do not have to guess very long what his answer would be. But ask him whether he thinks it would be possible for him to overcome his love of life, however great it may be, if his sovereign threatened him with the same sudden death unless he made a false deposition against an honorable man whom the ruler wished to destroy under a plausible pretext. Whether he would or not he perhaps will not venture to say; but that it would be possible for him he would certainly admit without hesitation. He judges, therefore, that he can do something because he knows that he ought, and he recognizes that he is free — a fact which, without the moral law, would have remained unknown to him.

§7. *Fundamental Law of Pure Practical Reason*

So act that the maxim of your will could always hold at the same time as the principle giving universal law.

REMARK

Pure geometry has postulates as practical pro- [31] positions, which, however, contain nothing more than the presupposition that one *can* do something and that, when some result is needed, one *should* do it; these are the only propositions of pure geometry that deal with an existing thing. They are thus practical rules under a problematic condition of the will. Here, however, the rule says: One ought absolutely to act in a certain way. The practical rule is therefore unconditional and thus is thought of a priori as a categorically practical proposition. The practical rule, which is thus here a law, absolutely and directly determines the will objectively, for pure reason, practical in itself, is here directly law-giving. The will is thought of as independent of empirical conditions and consequently as pure will, determined by the mere form of law, and this ground of determination is regarded as the supreme condition of all maxims.

The thing is strange enough and has no parallel in the remainder of practical knowledge. For the a priori thought of the possibility of giving universal law, which is thus merely problematic, is unconditionally commanded as a law without borrowing anything from experience or from any external will. It is, however, not a prescription according to which an act should occur in order to make a desired effect possible, for such a rule is always physically conditioned; it is, on the contrary, a rule which determines the will a priori only with respect to the form of its maxims. Therefore, it is at least not impossible to conceive of a law that alone serves the purpose of the *subjective* form of principles and yet is a ground of determination by virtue of the *objective* form of a law in general. The consciousness of this fundamental law may be called a fact of reason, since one cannot ferret it out from antecedent data of reason, such as the consciousness of freedom (for this is not antecedently given), and since it forces itself upon us as a synthetic proposition a priori based on no pure or empirical intuition. It would be analytic if the freedom of the will were presupposed, but for this, as a positive concept, an intellectual intuition would be needed, and here we cannot assume it. In order to regard this law without any misinterpretation as given, one must note that it is not an empirical fact but the sole fact of pure reason, which by it proclaims itself as originating law (*sic volo, sic iubeo*).[2]

COROLLARY

Pure reason alone is practical of itself, and it gives (to man) a universal law, which we call the *moral law*.

REMARK

The fact just mentioned is undeniable. One need [32] only analyze the sentence which men pass upon the lawfulness of their actions to see in every case that their reason, incorruptible and self-constrained, in every action holds up the maxim of the will to the pure will, i.e., to itself regarded as a priori practical; and this it does regardless of what inclination may say to the contrary. Now this principle of morality, on account of the universality of its legislation which makes it the formal supreme determining ground of the will regardless of any subjective differences among men, is declared by reason to be a law for all rational beings in so far as they have a will, i.e., faculty of determining their causality through the representation of a rule, and consequently in so far as they are competent to determine their actions according to principles and thus to act according to practical a priori principles, which alone have the necessity which reason demands in a principle. It is thus not limited to human beings but extends to all finite beings having reason and will; indeed, it includes the Infinite Being as the supreme intelligence. In the former case, however, the law has the form of an imperative. For though we can suppose that men as rational beings have a pure will, since they are affected by wants and sensuous motives we cannot suppose them to have a holy will, a will incapable of any maxims which conflict with the moral law. The moral law for them, therefore, is an imperative, commanding categorically because it is unconditioned. The relation of such a will to this law is one of dependence under the name of "obligation." This term implies a constraint to an ac-

[2]An allusion to Juvenal *Satire* vi: "What I will I decree as law."

tion, though this constraint is only that of reason and its objective law. Such an action is called [a] *duty*, because a pathologically affected (though not pathologically determined—and thus still free) choice involves a wish arising from subjective causes, and consequently such a choice often opposes pure objective grounds of determination. Such a will is therefore in need of the moral constraint of the resistance offered by practical reason, which may be called an inner but intellectual compulsion. In the supremely self-sufficing intelligence choice is correctly thought of as incapable of having any maxim that could not at the same time be objectively a law, and the concept of holiness, which is applied to it for this reason, elevates it not indeed above all practical laws but above all practically restrictive laws, and thus above obligation and duty. This holiness of will is, however, a practical Idea which must necessarily serve as a model which all finite rational beings must strive toward even though they cannot reach it. The pure moral law, which is itself for this reason called holy, constantly and rightly holds it before their eyes. The utmost that finite practical reason can accomplish is to make sure of the unending progress of its maxims toward this model and of the constancy of the finite rational being in making continuous progress. This is virtue, [33] and as a naturally acquired faculty, it can never be perfect, because assurance in such a case never becomes apodictic certainty, and as a mere pretense it is very dangerous.

§8. *Theorem IV*

The *autonomy* of the will is the sole principle of all moral laws and of the duties conforming to them; *heteronomy* of choice, on the other hand, not only does not establish any obligation but is opposed to the principle of obligation and to the morality of the will.

The sole principle of morality consists in independence from all material of the law (i.e., a desired object) and in the accompanying determination of choice by the mere form of giving universal law which a maxim must be capable of having. That independence, however, is freedom in the negative sense, while this intrinsic legislation of pure and thus practical reason is freedom in the positive sense. Therefore, the moral law expresses nothing else than the autonomy of pure practical reason, i.e., freedom. This autonomy or freedom is itself the formal condition of all maxims, under which alone they can all agree with the supreme practical law. If, therefore, the material of volition, which cannot be other than an object of desire which is connected to the law, comes into the practical law *as a condition of its possibility*, there results heteronomy of choice, or dependence on natural laws in following some impulse or inclination; it is heteronomy because the will does not give itself the law but only directions for a reasonable obedience to pathological laws. The maxim, however, which for this reason can never contain in itself the form of prescribing universal law, not only produces no obligation but is itself opposed to the principle of pure practical reason and thus also to the moral disposition, even though the action which comes from it may conform to the law.

REMARK I

Thus a practical precept which presupposes a material [34] and therefore empirical condition must never be reckoned a practical law. For the law of pure will, which is free, puts the will in a sphere entirely different from the empirical, and the necessity which it expresses, not being a natural necessity, can consist only in the formal conditions of the possibility of a law in general. All the material of practical rules rests only on subjective conditions, which can afford the rules no universality for rational beings (except a merely conditioned one as in the case where I desire this or that, and then there is something which I must do in order to get it). Without exception, they all revolve about the principle of one's own happiness. *Now it is certainly undeniable that every volition must have an object and therefore a material;*[3] but the material cannot be sup-

[3] The italics of this clause, which belies the most common misunderstanding of Kant's ethics, is justified by its importance, though in the German text it is in normal type.

posed, for this reason, to be the determining ground and condition of the maxim. If it were, the maxim could not be presented as giving universal law, because then the expectation of the existence of the object would be the determining cause of the choice, the dependence of the faculty of desire on the existence of some thing would have to be made basic to volition, and this dependence would have to be sought out in empirical conditions and therefore never could be a foundation of a necessary and universal rule. Thus the happiness of others may be the object of the will of a rational being, but if it were the determining ground of the maxim, not only would one have to presuppose that we find in the welfare of others a natural satisfaction but also one would have to find a want such as that which is occasioned in some men by a sympathetic disposition. This want, however, I cannot presuppose in every rational being, certainly not in God. The material of the maxim can indeed remain but cannot be its condition, for then it would not be fit for a law. The mere form of a law, which limits its material, must be a condition for adding this material to the will but not presuppose the material as the condition of the will. Let the material content be, for example, my own happiness. If I attribute this to everyone, as in fact I may attribute it to all finite beings, it can become an objective practical law only if I include within it the happiness of others. Therefore, the law that we should further the happiness of others arises not from the presupposition that this law is an object of everyone's choice but from the fact that the form of universality, which reason requires as condition for giving to the maxim of self-love the objective validity of law, is itself the determining ground of the will. Therefore not the object, i.e., the happiness of others, was the determining ground of the pure will but rather it was the lawful form alone. Through it I restricted my maxim, founded on inclination, by giving it the universality of a law, thus making it conformable [35] to pure practical reason. From this limitation alone, and not from the addition of any external drive, the concept of obligation arises to extend the maxim of self-love also to the happiness of others.

REMARK II

When one's own happiness is made the determining ground of the will, the result is the direct opposite of the principle of morality; and I have previously shown that, whenever the determining ground which is to serve as a law is located elsewhere than in the legislative form of the maxim, we have to reckon with this result. This conflict is not, however, merely logical, as is that between empirically conditioned rules which someone might nevertheless wish to erect into necessary principles of knowledge; it is rather a practical conflict, and, were the voice of reason with respect to the will not so distinct, so irrepressible, and so clearly audible to even the commonest man, it would drive morality to ruin. It can maintain itself only in the perplexing speculations of the schools which have temerity enough to close their ears to that heavenly voice in order to uphold a theory that costs no brainwork.

Suppose that an acquaintance whom you otherwise liked were to attempt to justify himself before you for having borne false witness by appealing to what he regarded as the holy duty of consulting his own happiness and, then, by recounting all the advantages he had gained thereby, pointing out the prudence he had shown in securing himself against detection, even by yourself, to whom alone he now reveals the secret only in order that he may be able at any time to deny it. And suppose that he then affirmed, in all seriousness, that he had thereby fulfilled a true human duty — you would either laugh in his face or shrink from him in disgust, even though you would not have the least grounds for objecting to such measures if someone regulated his principles solely with a view to his own advantage. Or suppose someone recommends to you as steward a man to whom you could blindly trust your affairs and, in order to inspire you with confidence, further extols him as a prudent man who has a masterly understanding of his own interest and is so indefatigably active that he misses no opportunity to further it; furthermore, lest you should be afraid of finding a vulgar selfishness in him, he praises the good taste with which he lives, not seeking his pleasure in making money or in coarse wantonness, but in the increase of his knowledge, in instructive conversation with a select circle, and even in relieving the needy. But, he adds, he is not particular as to the means (which, of course, derive their value only from the end), being as willing to use another's money and property as his own, pro- [36] vided only that he knows he can do so safely and without discovery. You would believe that the person making such a recommendation was either mocking you or had lost his mind. So distinct and sharp are the boundaries between morality and self-love that even the commonest eye cannot fail to distinguish whether a thing belongs to the one or the other. The few remarks which follow may appear superfluous where the truth is so obvious, but they serve at least to furnish somewhat greater distinctness to the judgment of common sense.

The principle of happiness can indeed give maxims, but never maxims which are competent to be laws of the will, even if universal happiness were made the object. For, since the knowledge of this rests on mere data of experience, as each judgment concerning it depends very much on the very changeable opinion of each person, it can give general but never universal rules; that is, the rules it gives will on the average be most often the right ones for this purpose, but they will not be rules which must hold always and necessarily. Consequently, no practical laws can be based on this principle. Since here an object of choice is made the basis of the rule and therefore must precede it, the rule cannot be founded upon or related to anything other than what one approves; and thus it refers to and is based on experience. Hence the variety of judgment must be infinite. This principle, therefore, does not prescribe the same practical rules to all rational beings, even though all the rules go under the same name — that of happiness. The moral law, however, is thought of as objectively necessary only because it holds good for everyone having reason and will.

The maxim of self-love (prudence) merely advises; the law of morality commands. Now there is a great difference between that which we are advised to do and that which we are obligated to do.

What is required in accordance with the principle of autonomy of choice is easily and without hesitation seen by the commonest intelligence; what is to be done under the presupposition of its heteronomy is hard to see and requires knowledge of the world. That is to say, what duty is, is plain of itself to everyone, but what is to bring true, lasting advantage to our whole existence is veiled in impenetrable obscurity, and much prudence is required to adapt the practical rule based upon it even tolerably to the ends of life by making suitable exceptions to it. But the moral law commands the most unhesitating obedience from everyone; consequently, the decision as to what is to be done in accordance with it must not be so difficult that even the commonest and most unpracticed understanding without any worldly prudence should go wrong in making it.

It is always in everyone's power to satisfy the commands of the categorical command of morality; this is but seldom [37] possible with respect to the empirically conditioned precept of happiness, and it is far from being possible, even in respect to a single purpose, for everyone. The reason is that in the former it is only a question of the maxim, which must be genuine and pure, but in the latter it is also a question of capacity and physical ability to realize a desired object. A command that everyone should seek to make himself happy would be foolish, for no one commands another to do what he already invariably wishes to do. One must only prescribe to him the rules for achieving his goal, or, better, provide him the means, for he is not able to do all that he wants to do. But to command morality under the name of duty is very reasonable, for its precept will not, for one thing, be willingly obeyed by everyone when it is in conflict with his inclinations. Then, regarding the means of obeying this law, there is no need to teach them, for in this respect whatever he wills to do he also can do.

He who has lost at play may be vexed at himself and his imprudence; but when he is conscious of having cheated at play, even though he has won, he must despise himself as soon as he compares himself with the moral law. This must therefore be something other than the principle of one's own happiness. For to have to say to himself, "I am a worthless man, though I've filled my purse," he must have a criterion of judgment different from that by which he approves of himself and says, "I am a prudent man, for I've enriched my treasure."

Finally, there is something else in the idea of our practical reason which accompanies transgression of a moral law, namely, its culpability. Becoming a partaker in happiness cannot be united with the concept of punishment as such. For even though he who punishes can do so with the benevolent intention of directing this punishment to this end, it must nevertheless be justified as punishment, i.e., as mere harm in itself, so that even the punished person, if it stopped there and he could see no glimpse of kindness behind the harshness, would yet have to admit that justice had been done and that his reward perfectly fitted his behavior. In every punishment as such there must first be justice, and this constitutes the essence of the concept. With it benevolence may, of course, be associated, but the person who deserves punishment has not the least reason to count on it. Punishment is physical harm which, even if not bound as a natural consequence to the morally bad, ought to be bound to it as a consequence according to principles of moral legislation. Now if every crime, without regard to the physical consequences to him who commits it, is punishable, i.e., involves a forfeiture of happiness at least in part, it is obviously absurd to say that the crime consists just in the fact that one has brought punishment upon himself and thus has injured his own happiness (which, according to the principle of [38] self-love, must be the correct concept of all crime). In this way, the punishment would be the reason for calling anything a crime, and justice would consist in withholding all punishment and even hindering natural punishment, for there would be no longer any evil in an action if the harm which would otherwise follow upon it and because of which alone the action was called evil would now be averted. To look upon all punishment and reward as machinery in the hand of a higher power, which by this means sets rational beings in action toward their final purpose (happiness), so obviously reduces the will to a mechanism destructive of freedom that it need not detain us.

More refined, but equally untrue, is the pretense of those who assume a certain particular moral sense which, instead of reason, determines the moral law, and in accordance with which the consciousness of virtue is directly associated with satisfaction and enjoyment, while consciousness of vice is associated with mental restlessness and pain. Thus everything is reduced to the desire for one's own happiness. Without repeating what has already been said, I will only indicate the fallacy they fall into. In order to imagine the vicious person as tormented with mortification by the consciousness of his transgressions, they must presuppose that he is, in the core of his character, at least to a certain degree morally good, just as they have to think of the person who is gladdened by the consciousness of doing dutiful acts as already virtuous. Therefore, the concept of morality and duty must precede all reference to this satisfaction and cannot be derived from it. One must already value the importance of what we call duty, the respect for the moral law, and the immediate worth which a person obtains in his own eyes through obedience to it, in order to feel satisfaction in the consciousness of his conformity to law or the bitter remorse which accompanies his awareness that he has transgressed it. Therefore, this satisfaction or spiritual unrest cannot be felt prior to the knowledge of obligation, nor can it be made the basis of the latter. One must be at least halfway honest even to be able to have an idea of these feelings. For the rest, as the human will by virtue of its freedom is directly determined by the moral law, I am far from denying that frequent practice in accordance with this determining ground can itself finally cause a subjective feeling of satisfaction. Indeed, it is a duty to establish and cultivate this feeling, which alone deserves to be called the moral feeling. But the concept of duty cannot be derived from it, for we would have to presuppose a feeling for law as such and regard as an object of sensation what can [39] only be thought by reason. If this did not end up in the flattest contradiction, it would destroy every concept of duty and fill its place with a merely mechanical play of refined inclinations, sometimes contending with the coarser.

If we now compare our supreme formal principle of pure practical reason, that of the autonomy of will, with all previous material principles of morality, we can exhibit them in a table which exhausts all possible cases except the one formal principle; thus we can show visually that it is futile to look around for another principle than the one presented here. All possible determining grounds of the will are either merely subjective and therefore empirical or objective and rational; in either case they may be external or internal.

Practical material determining grounds in the principle of morality are: [40]

SUBJECTIVE

EXTERNAL:	INTERNAL:
Education (Montaigne) Civil Constitution (Mandeville)	Physical Feeling (Epicurus) Moral Feeling (Hutcheson)

OBJECTIVE

INTERNAL:	EXTERNAL:
Perfection (Wolff and the Stoics)	Will of God (Crusius and other theological moralists)[4]

Those in the first group are without exception empirical and are obviously unfit for being the supreme principle of mor- [41] ality. Those in the second, however, are based on reason, for

[4]The authors referred to are Michèle de Montaigne, Bernard de Mandeville (*Inquiry into Moral Virtue*, 1723), Francis Hutcheson (*Inquiry Concerning the Original of Our Ideas of Virtue or Moral Goodness*, 1725), Christian Wolff (*Ontologia* §128), and Christian August Crusius (*Anweisung, Vernünftig zu Leben*, 1744).

perfection, as a character of things, and the highest perfection thought of in substance, i.e., God, can be thought of only through concepts of reason. The first concept, perfection, can be taken in either a theoretical or a practical sense. In the former, it means nothing more than the perfection of anything in its own kind (transcendental perfection), or the perfection of a thing merely as a thing generally (metaphysical perfection); and we need not discuss these here. The concept of perfection in its practical meaning, however, is the fitness or sufficiency of a thing to any kind of ends. This perfection, as a characteristic of man and thus as internal, is nothing else than talent, or skill, which strengthens or completes talent. The supreme perfection in substance, i.e., God (hence external), when regarded practically, is the sufficiency of this Being to all ends in general. Only if ends are already given can the concept of perfection in relation to them (either internal perfection in ourselves or external perfection of God) be the determining ground of the will. An end, however, as an object which precedes and contains the ground of determination of the will by a practical rule — that is, an end as the material of the will — is, if taken as a determining ground of the will, only empirical; it could thus serve for the Epicurean principle in the happiness theory but never as a pure rational principle of ethics and duty. Thus talents and their cultivation, because they contribute to the advantages of life, or the will of God, if agreement with it (without any practical principle independent of this Idea) be taken as an object of the will, can be motives only by reason of the happiness expected from them.

From these considerations, it follows, first, that all the principles exhibited here are material, and, second, that they include all possible material principles. Finally, since it was shown that all material principles were wholly unfit to be the supreme moral law, it follows that the formal practical principle of pure reason — according to which the mere form of a universal legislation, which is possible through our maxims, must constitute the supreme and direct determining ground of the will — is the only principle which can possibly furnish categorical imperatives, i.e., practical laws which enjoin actions as duty. Only a so-defined principle can serve as a principle of morality, whether in judging conduct or in applying it to the human will in determining it.

I. OF THE DEDUCTION OF THE PRINCIPLES OF PURE PRACTICAL REASON

This Analytic proves that pure reason can be prac- [42] tical, i.e., that of itself and independently of everything empirical it can determine the will. This it does through a fact wherein pure reason shows itself actually to be practical. This fact is autonomy in the principle of morality by which reason determines the will to action.

At the same time it shows this fact to be inextricably bound up with the consciousness of freedom of the will, and actually to be identical with it. By this freedom the will of a rational being, as belonging to the sensuous world, recognizes itself to be, like all other efficient causes, necessarily subject to the laws of causality, while in practical matters, in its other aspect as [a] being in itself, it is conscious of its existence as determinable in an intelligible order of things. It is conscious of this not by virtue of a particular intuition of itself but because of certain dynamic laws which determine its causality in the world of sense, for it has been sufficiently proved in another place[5] that if freedom is attributed to us, it transfers us into an intelligible order of things.

Now, if we compare the analytical part of the *Critique of Pure* (speculative) *Reason* with this Analytic, a noteworthy contrast between them appears. In that other *Critique*, not principles but pure sensible intuition (space and time) was the first datum which made a priori knowledge possible, though only of objects of the senses. Synthetical principles could not be derived from mere concepts without intuition; rather, these

[5] *Foundations of the Metaphysics of Morals* second edition (New York: Macmillan), pp. 70 ff.

principles could exist only in relation to sensible intuition and thus only in relation to objects of possible experience, since it is only the concepts of the understanding united with this intuition which can make that knowledge possible which we call experience. Beyond objects of experience, i.e., concerning things as noumena, all positive knowledge was correctly denied to speculative reason. This reason, however, was successful to the extent that it established with certainty the concept of noumena, i.e., it established the possibility—indeed, the necessity—of thinking of them. For example, it showed against all objections that the assumption of freedom, negatively considered, was entirely compatible with those principles and limitations of pure theoretical reason. But it could not give us anything definite to enlarge our knowledge of [43] such objects; rather it cut off any such prospect altogether.

On the other hand, the moral law, although it gives no such prospect, does provide a fact absolutely inexplicable from any data of the world of sense or from the whole compass of the theoretical use of reason, and this fact points to a pure intelligible world—indeed, it defines it positively and enables us to know something of it, namely, a law.

This law gives to the world of the senses, as sensuous nature (which concerns rational beings), the form of an intelligible world, i.e., the form of supersensuous nature, without interfering with the mechanism of sensuous nature. Nature, in the widest sense of the word, is the existence of things under laws. The sensuous nature of rational beings in general is their existence under empirically conditioned laws, and therefore it is, from the point of view of reason, heteronomy. The supersensuous nature of the same beings, on the other hand, is their existence according to laws which are independent of all empirical conditions and which therefore belong to the autonomy of pure reason. And since the laws, according to which the existence of things depends on cognition, are practical laws, supersensuous nature, so far as we can form a concept of it, is nothing else than nature under the autonomy of the pure practical reason. The law of this autonomy is the moral law, and it, therefore, is the fundamental law of supersensuous nature and of a pure world of the understanding, whose counterpart must exist in the world of sense without interfering with the laws of the latter. The former could be called the archetypal world (*natura archetypa*) which we know only by reason; the latter, on the other hand, could be called the ectypal world (*natura ectypa*), because it contains the possible effect of the Idea of the former as the determining ground of the will. For, in fact, the moral law ideally transfers us into a nature in which reason would bring forth the highest good were it accompanied by sufficient physical capacities; and it determines our will to confer on the sensuous world the form of a system of rational beings. The least attention to ourself shows that this Idea really stands as a model for the determination of our will.

When the maxim according to which I intend to give [44] testimony is tested by practical reason, I always inquire into what it should be if it were to hold as a universal law of nature. It is obvious that, in this way of looking at it, it would oblige everyone to truthfulness. For it cannot hold as a universal law of nature that an assertion should have the force of evidence and yet be intentionally false. Also the maxim which I adopt in respect to freely disposing of my life is at once determined when I inquire what it would have to be in order that a system of nature could maintain itself in accordance with such a law. Obviously in such a system of nature no one could choose to end his life, for such an arrangement could not constitute a permanent natural order. And so in all other cases.

Now, however, in actual nature as an object of experience, the free will is not of itself determined to follow such maxims as could of themselves establish a nature based on universal laws, or even such maxims as would fit into a system of nature so constituted; rather, its maxims are private inclinations, which form a natural whole according to pathological (physical) laws, but not a system of nature which is possible only through our will acting according to pure practical laws. However, through reason we are conscious of a law to which all our maxims are subject as though through our will a natural order must arise. Therefore, this law must be the Idea of a supersensuous nature, a nature not empirically given yet possible through freedom; to this nature we give objective reality, at least in a practical context, because we regard it as the object of our will as pure rational beings.

The difference, therefore, between the laws of a system of nature to which the will is subject and of a system of nature which is subject to a will (as far as the relation of the will to its free actions is concerned) rests on this: in the former, the objects must be the causes of the conceptions which determine the will, and in the latter, the will is the cause of the objects. Consequently, in the latter the causality of the objects has its determining ground solely in the pure faculty of reason, which therefore may be called pure practical reason.

There are, therefore, two very different problems. The first is: How can pure reason know objects a priori? The second is: How can pure reason be a directly determining ground of the will, i.e., of the causality of a rational being with res- [45] pect to the reality of the objects, merely through the thought of the universal validity of its own maxims as a law?

The first of these questions belongs to the *Critique of Pure* (speculative) *Reason*; it requires that we first show how intuitions, without which no object can be given and without which none can be known synthetically, are possible a priori. Its answer lies in the fact that intuitions are without exception sensible, and therefore no speculative knowledge is possible which reaches further than possible experience; consequently, all principles of pure speculative reason avail only to make possible experience of objects which are actually given or of objects which though they may be given *ad infinitum* are never completely given.

The second question belongs to the *Critique of Practical Reason*. It requires no explanation of how objects of the faculty of desire are possible, for that, as a task of the theoretical knowledge of nature, is left to the *Critique of Pure* (speculative) *Reason*. It asks only how reason can determine the maxim of the will, whether this occurs only by means of empirical representations as determining grounds, or whether even pure reason might be practical and might be a law of a possible but not empirically knowable order of nature. The possibility of such a supersensuous nature, the concept of which can be the ground of its reality through our free will, requires no a priori intuition of an intelligible world, which even in this case would be impossible to us, since it is supersensuous. For it is only a question of the determining ground of volition in its own maxims: Is the determining ground empirical or is it a concept of pure reason (a concept of its lawfulness in general)? And how can it be the latter? The decision as to whether the causality of the will is sufficient to make its objects real is left up to the theoretical principles of reason, involving as it does an investigation of the possibility of objects of volition, the intuition of which is no component of the practical problem. The only concern here is with the determination of the will and with the determining ground of its maxims as a free will, not with its result. For if the will be only in lawful accord with pure reason, the will's power in execution may be what it may; and a system of nature [46] may or may not actually arise according to these maxims of the legislation of a possible nature — all this does not trouble us in this *Critique*, which concerns itself only with whether and how reason can be practical, i.e., whether and how it can directly determine the will.

In this inquiry no objection can be raised that the *Critique* begins with pure practical laws and their reality. Instead of intuition, it makes the concept of their existence in the intelligible world, i.e., freedom, its foundation. For this concept has no other meaning, and these laws are possible only in relation to the freedom of the will; but, if the will is presupposed as free, then they are necessary. Conversely, freedom is necessary because those laws are necessary, being practical postulates. How this consciousness of the moral laws or — what amounts to the same thing — how this consciousness of freedom is possible cannot be further explained; its permissibility, however, is established in the theoretical *Critique*.

The exposition of the supreme principle of practical reason

is now finished. It has shown, first, what it contains, and that it is of itself entirely a priori and independent of empirical principles; and then it has shown how it differs from all other practical principles. With the deduction, i.e., the justification of its objective and universal validity and the discernment of the possibility of such a synthetic a priori proposition, one cannot hope to have everything as easy as it was with the principles of pure theoretical understanding. For the latter referred to objects of possible experience, i.e., appearances, and it could be proved that they could be known as objects of experience and, consequently, that all possible experience must be conformable to these laws, only because these appearances, in accordance with these laws, could be brought under the categories. Such a procedure, however, I cannot follow in the deduction of the moral law. For the moral law does not concern knowledge of the properties of objects, which may be given to reason from some other source; rather, it concerns knowledge in so far as it can itself become the ground of the existence of objects, and in so far as reason, by virtue of this same knowledge, has causality in a rational being. The moral law is concerned with pure reason, regarded as a faculty directly determining the will.

But human insight is at an end as soon as we arrive [47] at fundamental powers or faculties, for their possibility can in no way be understood and yet should not be just arbitrarily imagined or assumed. Therefore in the theoretical use of reason only experience could justify their assumption. Such empirical proof, as a substitute for deduction from sources of knowledge a priori, is, however, denied with respect to the pure practical faculty of reason. For whatever needs to draw the evidence of its reality from experience must depend for the grounds of its possibility on principles of experience; by its very notion, however, pure yet practical reason cannot be held to be dependent in this way. Moreover, the moral law is given, as an apodictically certain fact, as it were, or pure reason, a fact of which we are a priori conscious, even if it be granted that no example could be found in which it has been followed exactly. Thus the objective reality of the moral law can be

proved through no deduction, through no exertion of the theoretical, speculative, or empirically supported reason; and, even
if one were willing to renounce its apodictic certainty, it could
not[6] be confirmed by any experience and thus proved a poster-
iori. Nevertheless, it is firmly established of itself.

Instead of this vainly sought deduction of the moral principle, however, something entirely different and unexpected appears: the moral principle itself serves as a principle of the deduction of an inscrutable faculty which no experience can
prove but which speculative reason had to assume as at least
possible (in order not to contradict itself in finding among its
cosmological Ideas something unconditional in its causality).
This is the faculty of freedom, which the moral law, itself needing no justifying grounds, shows to be not only possible but actual in beings who acknowledge the law as binding upon them.
The moral law is, in fact, a law of causality through freedom and
thus a law of the possibility of a supersensuous nature, just as
the metaphysical law of events in the world of sense was a law
of the causality of sensible nature; the moral law thus defines
that which speculative philosophy had to leave undefined.
That is, it defines the law for a causality the concept of which
was only negative in speculative philosophy, and for the first
time it gives objective reality to this concept.

This kind of credential for the moral law, namely, that [48]
it is itself demonstrated to be a principle of the deduction of
freedom as a causality of pure reason, is a sufficient substitute
for any a priori justification, since theoretical reason had to assume at least the possibility of freedom in order to fill one of its
own needs. For the moral law sufficiently proves its reality
even for the *Critique of Pure* (speculative) *Reason* by giving a
positive definition to a causality thought merely negatively, the
possibility of which was incomprehensible to speculative reason though this reason was compelled to assume it. The moral
law adds to the negative concept a positive definition, that of a
reason which determines the will directly through the condi-

[6]"Not" inserted by Vorländer.

tion of a universal lawful form of the maxims of the will. Thus reason, which with its Ideas always became transcendent when proceeding in a speculative manner, can be given for the first time an objective, although still only practical, reality; its transcendent use is changed into an immanent use, whereby reason becomes, in the field of experience, an efficient cause through Ideas.

The determination of the causality of beings in the world of sense as such can never be unconditioned, and yet for every series of conditions there must be something unconditioned, and consequently a causality which is entirely self-determining. Therefore, the Idea of freedom as a faculty of absolute spontaneity was not just a desideratum but, as far as its possibility was concerned, an analytical principle of pure speculative reason. But because it is absolutely impossible to give an example of it from experience, since no absolutely unconditioned determination of causality can be found among the causes of things as appearances, we could defend the supposition of a freely acting cause when applied to a being in the world of sense only in so far as that being was regarded also as noumenon. This defense was made by showing that it was not self-contradictory to regard all its actions as physically conditioned so far as they are appearances, and yet at the same time to regard their causality as physically unconditioned so far as the acting being is regarded as a being of the understanding. Thus the concept of freedom is made the regulative principle of reason. I thereby do not indeed learn what the object may be to which this kind of causality is attributed. I do, however, remove the difficulty, since, on the one hand, in the explanation of natural occurrences, including the actions of rational beings, I leave to the mechanism of natural necessity the right to ascend from conditioned to condition *ad infinitum*, while, on [49] the other hand, I hold open for speculative reason the place which for it is vacant, i.e., the intelligible, in order to put the unconditioned in it. I could not, however, give content to this supposition, i.e., convert it into knowledge even of the possibility of a being acting in this way. Pure practical reason now

fills this vacant place with a definite law of causality in an intelligible world (causality through freedom). This is the moral
law. Speculative reason does not herewith grow in insight but
only in respect to the certitude of its problematic concept of
freedom, to which objective, though only practical, reality is
now indubitably given. Even the concept of causality, having its
application and hence significance only in relation to appearances which it connects into experiences (as shown in the *Critique of Pure Reason*), is not enlarged by this reality so as to extend its employment beyond these boundaries. For if reason
sought to go beyond them, it would have to show how the logical relation of ground and consequent could be synthetically
used with another kind of intuition than the sensible, i.e., it
would have to show how a *causa noumenon* is possible. This
reason cannot do, but as practical reason it does not concern itself with this demand, since it only posits the determining
ground of the causality of man as a sensuous being (this causality being given) in pure reason (which is therefore called practical); it does so not in order to know objects but only to define
causality in respect to objects in general. It can abstract the
concept of cause itself altogether from that application to objects which has theoretical knowledge as its purpose, since this
concept can always be found a priori in the understanding,
independently of any intuition. Thus reason uses this concept
only for a practical purpose, transferring the determining ground of the will to the intelligible order of things,
at the same time readily confessing that it does not understand how the concept of cause can be a condition of
knowledge of these things. Causality with respect to the
actions of the will in the world of sense must, of course, be
known by reason in a definite way, for otherwise practical
reason could produce no act. But the concept which reason
makes of its own causality as noumenon does not need [50]
to be determined theoretically for the purpose of knowing its
supersensible existence. Reason does not need to be able to
give it [cognitive] significance. Despite this, it acquires significance through the moral law, although only for practical use.

Even regarded theoretically, the concept remains always a pure concept of the understanding, given a priori, and applicable to objects whether given by the senses or not. If they are not sensibly given, however, the concept has no definite theoretical significance and application but is only the understanding's formal but nevertheless essential thought of an object in general. The significance which reason gives to it through the moral law is exclusively practical, since the Idea of the law of a causality (of the will) has causality itself or is its determining ground.

II. OF THE RIGHT OF PURE REASON TO AN
EXTENSION IN ITS PRACTICAL USE WHICH IS NOT
POSSIBLE TO IT IN ITS SPECULATIVE USE

In the moral principle as we have presented it there is a law of causality which puts the determining ground of causality above all conditions of the world of sense. We have thought of the will as determinable inasmuch as it belongs to an intelligible world and of the subject of this will (man) as belonging to a pure intelligible world, though in this relation man is unknown to us. (How this relation can be thought and yet be unknowable has been shown in the *Critique of Pure* (speculative) *Reason.*) We have, I say, *thought* of man and his will in this way and we have *defined* the will with respect to its causality by means of a law which cannot be counted among the natural laws of the world of sense; finally, we have thereby *widened* our knowledge beyond the boundaries of the world of sense. But this is a presumption which the *Critique of Pure Reason* declared to be void in all speculation. How, then, is the practical use of pure reason to be reconciled with its theoretical use in respect to determining the boundaries of their competence?

David Hume, who can be said to have begun the assault on the claims of pure reason which made a thorough examination of them necessary, argued as follows. The concept of [51] cause is one which involves the necessity of a connection between different existing things, in so far as they are different. Thus, when A is granted, I recognize that B, something entirely

different from it, must necessarily exist also. Necessity, however, can be attributed to a connection only so far as the connection is known a priori, for experience of a connection
would only give knowledge that it existed, not that it necessarily existed. Now it is impossible, he says, to know a priori and as
necessary the connection which holds between one thing and
another (or between one property and another entirely different from it) if this connection is not given in perception. Therefore, the concept of a cause is itself fraudulent and deceptive.
To speak in the mildest way, it is an illusion which is excusable
only since the custom (a subjective necessity) of frequently
perceiving certain things or their properties along with or in
succession to one another is insensibly taken for an objective
necessity of placing such a connection in the objects themselves. Thus the concept of cause has been acquired surrepti-
tiously and illegitimately—nay, it can never be acquired or
certified, because it demands a connection in itself void, chi-
merical, and untenable before reason, a connection to which
no object could ever correspond.

So first with reference to all knowledge which concerned the
existence of things (thus excepting mathematics), empiricism
was introduced as the exclusive source of principles; with it,
however, came the most unyielding skepticism with respect to
the whole science of nature (as philosophy). For on such principles we can never infer a consequence from the given properties of things as existing, for to such an inference there is
needed a concept of cause, a concept implying necessity in
such a connection; we can only expect, by the rule of imagination, similar cases, though this expectation is never certain no
matter how often it is fulfilled. Indeed, of no occurrence could
one say: something *must* have preceded it on which it *necessarily* followed, i.e., it must have had a *cause.* Thus, even if
one knew of such frequent cases in which this antecedent was
present that a rule could be derived from them, we could still
not assume that it happens this way always and necessarily.
Thus the rights of blind chance, with which all use of reason
ceases, must be admitted; this firmly and irrefutably establishes
skepticism toward all inferences from effects to causes. [52]

Mathematics at first escaped lightly because Hume thought that its propositions were analytical, i.e., proceeded from one property to another by virtue of identity and consequently according to the law of contradiction. This, however, is false; they are all synthetical. And though geometry, for example, has nothing to do with the existence of things but only with their a priori properties in a possible intuition, it nevertheless proceeds just as in the case of the causal concept, going from one property A to another entirely different property B necessarily connected with it. But even this science, so highly esteemed for its apodictic certainty, must finally succumb to empiricism with regard to its principles for the same reason that Hume substituted custom for objective necessity in the concept of cause. In spite of all its pride, it will have to acquiesce to this skepticism by lowering its bold claims demanding a priori assent, expecting approval of the universal validity of its theorems only because of the kindness of observers who, as witnesses, would not hesitate to admit that what the geometer propounds as axioms had always been perceived as facts, and that, consequently, they could be expected to be true in the future even though there was no necessity in them. In this way, Hume's empiricism leads inevitably to skepticism even with respect to mathematics and consequently in the entire theoretical scientific employment of reason (for this is either philosophy or mathematics). In view of the terrible overthrow of these chief branches of knowledge, whether ordinary reason will come through any better I leave to the judgment of each. It may be that it will rather become inextricably entangled in the same destruction of all knowledge, with the consequence that from the same principles there will result a universal skepticism, even though it concern only the learned.

My own labors in the *Critique of Pure Reason* were occasioned by Hume's skeptical teaching, but they went much further and covered the entire field of pure theoretical reason in its synthetic use, including what is generally called [53] metaphysics. I proceeded with reference to the doubts raised by the Scottish philosopher concerning the concept of causality as follows. I granted that, when Hume took the objects of experience as things in themselves (as is almost always done), he was entirely correct in declaring the concept of cause to be deceptive and an illusion; for it cannot be understood, with reference to things in themselves and their properties as such, why, if A is given, something else, B, must also necessarily be given. Thus he could not admit such a priori knowledge of things regarded as they are in themselves. This acute man could even less admit an empirical origin of the concept, for this would directly contradict the necessity of the connection which constitutes the essence of the concept of causality. Consequently, the concept was proscribed, and into its place stepped custom in observing the course of perceptions.

From my investigations, however, it resulted that the objects with which we have to do in experience are by no means things in themselves but only appearances. Furthermore, if we assume that they are things in themselves, it is impossible to see how, if A is granted, it would be contradictory not to grant B, which is altogether different from A. That is, it is impossible to see how it would be contradictory not to grant the necessity of the connection of A as cause with B as effect; but it is very understandable that A and B as appearances *in one experience* must necessarily be connected in a certain manner (e.g., with reference to their temporal relations) and that they cannot be separated without contradicting that connection by means of which experience is possible, in which experience they become objects and alone knowable to us. This was actually the case, so that I could not only prove the objective reality of the concept of cause with reference to objects of experience but also *deduce* it as an a priori concept because of the necessity of the connection it implies. That is, I could show its possibility from pure understanding without any empirical sources. So, after banishing empiricism from its origin, I was able to overthrow its inevitable consequence, skepticism, first, in natural science and, then, in mathematics, both of which sciences have reference to objects of possible experience, and in both of which skepticism has the same grounds. Thus I re- [54]

moved the radical doubt of whatever theoretical reason professes to discern.

But how lies it with reference to the application of this category of causality (and similarly of all the others, for without them there can be no knowledge of existing things) to things which are not objects of possible experience but lie beyond its boundaries? For it must be remembered that I could deduce the objective reality of these concepts only with reference to objects of possible experience. But the very fact that I have saved them only in this one case and that I have shown that by virtue of them objects may be thought though not determined a priori — this fact gives them a place in pure understanding from which they are referred to objects in general, whether sensible or not. If anything is lacking, it is the conditions for the application of these categories, and especially that of causality, to objects. This condition is intuition, and, where it is lacking, this application for the purpose of theoretical *knowledge* of the object as noumenon is rendered impossible. This knowledge is absolutely forbidden (even in the *Critique of Pure Reason*) to anyone who ventures upon it. Still, the objective reality of the concept remains and can even be used with reference to noumena, though the concept is not in the least theoretically determined, and no knowledge can be effected with it. That this concept, even in relation to a [supersensible] object, contains nothing impossible was proved by the fact that [even] in its application to objects of the senses its seat in the pure understanding remained assured. And if, when subsequently applied to things in themselves which cannot be objects of experience, it cannot be determined so as to represent a definite object for the purposes of theoretical cognition, it could nevertheless be determined for application to some other purpose, such as the practical. This would not be so if, as Hume asserted, the concept of causality contained something inconceivable.

In order to discover the condition for applying the concept in question to noumena, we need only to refer back to the reason why we are not satisfied with applying it to objects of experience but wish also to apply it to things in themselves. It soon appears that it is not a theoretical but a practical purpose which makes it a necessity for us. In speculation, even if we [55] were successful [in this new application], we should still have made no true gain in the knowledge of nature or of any given objects; but we should have taken a long step from the sensibly conditioned (in which we have already enough to do to remain and industriously to follow the chain of causes) to the super-sensible in order to complete our knowledge of its foundations and to fix its boundaries. But there always remains an infinite unfilled chasm between that boundary and what we know, and [in taking such a step] we should have hearkened to a vain curiosity instead of acting from a sober desire for knowledge.

But besides the relationship which the understanding has to objects in theoretical knowledge, there is also the relationship in which it stands to the faculty of desire, which is therefore called the will, or the pure will in so far as the pure understanding (which in such a case is called reason) is practical through the mere representation of a law. The objective reality of a pure will or of a pure practical reason (they being the same) is given a priori in the moral law, as it were by a fact, for the latter term can be applied to a determination of the will which is inescapable, even though it does not rest on any empirical principles. In the concept of a will, however, the concept of causality is already contained; thus in that of a pure will there is the concept of causality with freedom, i.e., of a causality not determinable according to natural laws and consequently not susceptible to any empirical intuition as proof [of the reality of the free will]. Nevertheless, this concept completely justifies its objective reality in the pure practical law a priori, though it is easily seen that it is not for the purpose of the theoretical but solely for that of the practical use of reason. Now the concept of a being which has a free will is that of a *causa noumenon*; and we are assured that this concept does not contradict itself, because the concept of a cause originates exclusively in pure understanding, and its objective reality with reference to objects in general is guaranteed by the Deduction [in the *Critique of Pure Reason*]. As independent in origin from all sensible conditions, it is itself not to be restricted to phenomena; except when a definite theoretical use of it is to be made, it could certainly be applied to things as pure beings of the understanding. But because no intuition, which could only be sensible, can support this application, *causa noumenon* is, for the theoretical use of reason, an empty concept, although a possible and thinkable one. [56] Through it I do not strive to know theoretically the characteristic of a being in so far as it has a pure will; it is enough for me to denote it as such by means of this concept and thus to couple the concept of causality with that of freedom (and with what is inseparable from it, i.e., the moral law as its determining ground). I have this right by virtue of the pure nonempirical origin of the concept of cause, since I [here] make no other use of the concept than in relation to the moral law which determines its reality; that is, I hold that I am justified only in making a practical use of it.

Had I, with Hume, denied objective reality in the theoretical use to the concept of causality, not only in its reference to things in themselves (the supersensuous) but also in reference to objects of the senses, this concept would have lost all meaning, and as a theoretically impossible concept it would have been declared entirely worthless; and since that which is nothing lends itself to no use, the practical use of a theoretically null concept would have been absurd. The concept of an empirically unconditioned causality is indeed theoretically empty, since it has no appropriate intuition, even though it is still possible and refers to an indeterminate object; in compensation for this, the concept gains significance [not from a given object but] in the moral law and consequently in a practical relation. Even though I have no intuition which would determine its objective theoretical reality, it nevertheless has a real application exhibited *in concreto* in dispositions or maxims; that is, its practical reality can be pointed out. All this is sufficient to justify the concept even with respect to noumena.

This objective reality of a pure concept of the understanding in the field of the supersensible, once ushered in, gives objective reality to all the other categories, though only in so far as they stand in a necessary connection with the determining ground of the pure will (the moral law). This objective reality, however, is of only practical application, since it has not the slightest effect in enlarging theoretical knowledge of these objects as insight into their nature by pure reason. As we shall find in the sequel, these categories have reference only to beings as intelligences, and in them only to the relation of the reason to the will, and consequently only to the prac- [57] tical; further than that they pretend to no knowledge of them. Other characteristics belonging to the theoretical mode of conceiving of such supersensuous beings, and brought forward in connection with these categories, are not to be counted as knowledge but only as a right (for practical purposes, however, a necessity) to assume and presuppose them. This must be done even where one assumes a supersensible being (e.g., God) by analogy, i.e., by a purely rational relation of which we make practical use with reference to what is sensible. Thus the application of the categories to the supersensible, which occurs only from a practical point of view, gives to pure theoretical reason not the least encouragement to run riot into the transcendent.

CHAPTER II

THE CONCEPT OF AN OBJECT OF PURE PRACTICAL REASON

By a concept of an object of practical reason I understand the representation of an object as an effect possible through freedom. To be an object of practical knowledge as such signifies, therefore, only the relation of the will to the action whereby it or its opposite is brought into being. To decide whether or not something is an object of the *pure* practical reason is only to discern the possibility or impossibility of willing the action by which a certain object would be made actual, provided we had the ability to bring it about (the latter being a matter which experience must decide). If the object is taken as the determining ground of our faculty of desire, its physical possibility through the free use of our strength must precede the decision as to whether it is or is not an object of practical reason. But if, [58] on the other hand, the a priori law can be regarded as the determining ground of action, which is accordingly seen as determined by pure practical reason, then the judgment as to whether or not something is an object of pure practical reason is wholly independent of any question of our physical ability; the only question is whether we should will an action directed to the existence of an object if it were within our power. Consequently, the *moral possibility* of the action takes precedence, for in this case it is not the object but the law of the will which is the motive of the action.

The sole objects of a practical reason are thus those of *the good* and *the evil*. By the former, one understands a necessary object of the faculty of desire, and by the latter, a necessary object of aversion, both according to a principle of reason.

If the concept of the good is not derived from a practical law but rather serves as the ground of the latter, it can only be the concept of something whose existence promises pleasure and thereby determines the causality of the subject (the faculty of desire) to produce it. Now, because it is impossible to see a priori which representation will be accompanied with pleasure and which with pain, it would be solely a matter of experience to discern what is immediately good or evil. The property of the subject, by virtue of which such experience could be had, is the feeling of pleasure or displeasure as a receptivity belonging to inner sense; thus the concept of that which is immediately good would only refer to that with which the sensation of gratification is immediately associated, and the concept of the absolutely evil would have to be related only to that which directly excites pain.

Even the usage of language is opposed to this, however, since it distinguishes the pleasant from the good and the unpleasant from the evil, and demands that good and evil be judged by reason and thus through concepts which alone can be universally communicated, and not by mere sensation which is limited to individual subjects and their susceptibilities. For this reason, and also because pleasure or displeasure cannot be immediately associated a priori with a representation of an object, the philosopher who felt obliged to make a feeling of pleasure basic to his practical judgment would have to denominate "good" that which is a means to the pleasant, and "evil" that which is the cause of unpleasantness and pain, for judgment of the relation of means to end certainly belongs to reason. Although reason alone is capable of discerning the connection of means and intentions (so that the will could be defined as the faculty of purposes, since they are al- [59] ways determining grounds of the faculty of desire according to principles), the practical maxims which follow merely as means from the concept of the good never contain anything good in itself as the object of the will but only something good *for* something else. In this way the good would be only the useful, and that for which it is useful must always lie outside the will, in feeling [*Empfindung*]. If the latter, as pleasant feeling, had to be distinguished from the concept of the good, there would be nothing immediately good, and the good would have to be sought in the means to something else, i.e., some pleasantness.

There is an old formula of the schools:[1] *Nihil appetimus, nisi sub ratione boni; nihil aversamur, nisi sub ratione mali.* It is often used correctly, but often also in a manner very injurious to philosophy, since the expressions *boni* and *mali* contain an ambiguity due to the poverty of the [Latin] language. These words are capable of a double meaning and therefore inevitably bring practical laws into a precarious position; and philosophy, in using these expressions, becomes aware of the divergence of concepts associated with the same word even though it can find no special expressions for them, and is forced to sub-

---

[1] See Christian Wolff, *Psychologia rationalis* §§ 880, 881, 892; A. G. Baumgarten, *Metaphysica* § 665.

tle distinctions about which later agreement cannot be obtained, since the difference cannot be directly stated by any suitable expression.*

The German language has the good fortune to possess expressions which do not permit this difference to be overlooked. It has two very different concepts and equally different expressions for what the Latins named with the single word *bonum*. For *bonum*, it has *das Gute* [the good] and *das Wohl* [well-being]; for *malum, das Böse* [the evil, wicked] and *das Übel* [the bad, ill] or *das Weh* [woe]. Thus there are two very different judgments if in an action we have regard to its [60] goodness or wickedness or to our weal or woe. It follows just from this that the aforementioned psychological proposition is at least very doubtful if it is translated: "We desire nothing except with a view to our weal or woe." On the other hand, it is indubitably certain and at the same time clearly expressed when rendered: "We desire nothing, under the direction of reason, except in so far as we hold it to be good or evil."

"Well-being" or "woe" indicates only a relation to our state of pleasantness or unpleasantness, of enjoyment or pain; if for that reason we desire or avoid an object, we do so only in so far as it is related to our sensibility and to the feeling of pleasure or displeasure which it produces. But *good* or *evil* always indicates a relation to the will so far as it is determined by the law of reason to make something its object, for the will is never determined directly by the object and our representation of it; rather, the will is a faculty for making a rule of reason the motive of an action that can make an object real. Thus good or evil is properly referred to actions and not to the sensory state of the

---

*Moreover, the expression *sub ratione boni* is also ambiguous. For it can mean: we represent something to be good, if and because we desire (will) it. Or it can mean: we desire something, because we represent it to be good. Thus either the desire is the determining ground of the concept of the object as a good or the concept of the good is the determining ground of desire (will). In the first case, *sub ratione boni* would mean: we will something under the idea of the good; and in the second: we will something in consequence of this idea, which must precede volition as its determining ground.

person. If something is to be, or is held to be, absolutely good or evil in all respects and without qualification, it could not be a thing but only the manner of acting, i.e., it could be only the maxim of the will, and consequently the acting person himself as a good or evil person.

Though one may make fun of the Stoic who in the worst paroxysm of gout cried out, "Pain, however thou tormentest me, I will never admit that thou art anything evil (κακόν, *malum*)!" he was nevertheless right. He felt it was something bad, and he betrayed that in his cry; but that anything [morally] evil [*ein Böses*] attached to him he had no reason to concede, for the pain did not in the least diminish the worth of his person but only the worth of his condition. A single lie of which he was conscious would have struck down his pride, but pain served only as an occasion for raising it when he was conscious that he had not made himself liable to it by an unrighteous action and thus culpable.

What we call good must be, in the judgment of every reasonable man, an object of the faculty of desire, and evil [61] must be, in everyone's eyes, an object of aversion. Thus, in addition to sense, this judgment requires reason. So it is with truthfulness as opposed to a lie, with justice in contrast to violence, etc. But we can call something bad [*übel*], however, which everyone at the same time must acknowledge as good, either directly or indirectly. Whoever submits to a surgical operation feels it without doubt to be something bad, but by reason he and everyone else will declare it good. When, however, someone who delights in annoying and vexing peace-loving folk receives at last a right good beating, the beating is certainly a bad thing, but everyone approves of it and considers it as good in itself even if nothing further results from it; nay, even he who gets the beating must acknowledge, in his reason, that justice has been done to him, because he sees the connection between well-being and well-doing, which reason inevitably holds before him, here put into practice.

Certainly our weal and woe are *very important* in the estimation of our practical reason; and, as far as our nature as sensuous beings is concerned, our happiness is the *only* thing of importance, provided this is judged, as reason especially requires, not according to transitory sensation but according to the influence which this contingency has on our whole existence and our satisfaction with it. But still not everything depends upon that. Man is a being of needs, so far as he belongs to the world of sense, and to this extent his reason certainly has an inescapable responsibility from the side of his sensuous nature to attend to its interest and to form practical maxims with a view to the happiness of this and, where possible, of a future life. But still he is not so completely animal as to be indifferent to everything that reason says on its own and to use it merely as a tool for satisfying his needs as a sensuous being. That he has reason does not in the least raise him in worth above mere animality if reason serves only the purposes which, among animals, are taken care of by instinct; if this were so, reason would be only a specific way nature had made use of to equip man for the same purpose for which animals are qualified, without fitting him for any higher purpose. No doubt, as a result of this unique [62] arrangement, he needs reason, to consider at all times his weal and woe. But he has reason for a yet higher purpose, namely, to consider also what is in itself good or evil, which pure and sensuously disinterested reason alone can judge, and furthermore, to distinguish this estimation from a sensuous estimation and to make the former the supreme condition of the latter.

In this estimation of the difference between the good and evil as such and that which can be so called only with respect to well-being or ill, it is a question of the following points. Either: a principle of reason is thought of as already the determining ground of the will without reference to possible objects of the faculty of desire (and thus as a determining ground only through the lawful form of the maxim); then that principle is a practical law a priori, and pure reason is assumed to be in itself practical; the law directly determines the will; action in accordance with it is in itself good; and a will whose maxims always accord with this law is absolutely and in every respect good and the supreme condition of all good. Or: a determining ground of the faculty of desire precedes the maxim of the will, and this determining ground presupposes an object of pleasure or displeasure and consequently something that pleases or pains; in this case the maxim of reason, to pursue the former and to avoid the latter, determines actions which are good only with reference to our inclination and consequently only mediately good, being a means to a further purpose; and such maxims can never be called laws but only reasonable practical precepts. In the latter case, the end itself, the enjoyment we seek, is not a [moral] good but only well-being, not a concept of reason but an empirical concept of an object of sensation. Only the use of the means to it, i.e., the action, is called good (because reasonable deliberation is required for it). But, even so, the action is not absolutely good but good only in relation to our sensuous being and its feeling of pleasure or displeasure. The will whose maxims are affected by it is not a pure will, for the latter concerns itself only with that by which pure reason can of itself be practical.

This is the place for an explanation of the paradox of method in a critical examination of practical reason. The paradox is that the concept of good and evil is not defined prior to the [63] moral law, to which, it would seem, the former would have to serve as foundation; rather the concept of good and evil must be defined after and by means of the law. Even if we did not know that the principle of morality was a pure law determining the will a priori, we would nevertheless at the beginning have to leave it undecided whether the will has merely empirical or also pure determining grounds a priori. We would have to do this in order not to assume principles quite arbitrarily, since it is against all the basic rules of philosophical method to assume as already decided that which is the point in question. Assuming that we wished to begin with the concept of the good in order to derive the laws of the will from it, this concept of an object (as a good object) would designate this object as the sole determining ground of the will. But because this concept had no practical law a priori as its standard, the criterion of good or evil could be placed only in the agreement of the object with our feeling of pleasure or displeasure, and the use of reason could only consist in part in determining this pleasure or displeasure in connection with all the sensations of our existence and in part in determining the means of providing ourselves with the object of these feelings. Now, since only through experience can we find out what is in accordance with the feeling of pleasure, and since by hypothesis the practical law is to be based on it, the possibility of a priori practical laws is excluded because it was thought necessary first of all to find an object for the will the concept of which, as a good object, would have to constitute the universal though empirical determining ground of the will.

It was, on the contrary, necessary first to investigate whether there was not also an a priori determining ground of the will which could have been found nowhere except in a pure practical law (and indeed in this only in so far as its mere lawful form prescribed maxims without reference to an object). But because an object, according to concepts of good and evil, had been made the basis of every practical law, and because the object, in the absence of any prior law, could be thought only according to empirical concepts, the possibility was already removed even of conceiving a pure practical law. Had one previously analyzed the practical law, he would have found, on the contrary, not that the concept of the good as an object [64] of the moral law determines the latter and makes it possible, but rather the reverse, i.e., that the moral law is that which first defines the concept of the good — so far as it absolutely deserves this name — and makes it possible.

This remark, which refers only to the method of the deepest moral investigations, is important. It explains once and for all the reasons which occasion all the confusions of philosophers concerning the supreme principle of morals. For they sought an object of the will in order to make it into the material and the foundation of a law (which would then not be the directly determining ground of the will, but would be the determining ground of the will indirectly, only by means of that object referred to the feeling of pleasure or displeasure); instead, they should have first looked for a law that a priori and directly determined the will, and only then determined the object conformable to it. Whether they placed this object of pleasure, which was to deliver the supreme concept of the good, in happiness, or in perfection, in moral feeling, or in the will of God —their fundamental principle was always heteronomy, and they came inevitably to empirical conditions for a moral law. This was because they could call their object, as the direct determining ground of the will, good or bad only according to its exclusively empirical relation to feeling. Only a formal law, i.e., one which prescribes to reason nothing more than the form of its giving universal law as the supreme condition of maxims, can be a priori a determining ground of practical reason. The ancients openly revealed this error by devoting their ethical investigation entirely to the definition of the concept of the highest good and thus posited an object which they intended subsequently to make the determining ground of the will in the moral law. But only much later, when the moral law has been established by itself and justified as the direct determining ground of the will, can this object be presented to the will whose form now is determined a priori. This we shall undertake in the Dialectic of Pure Practical Reason. The moderns, among whom the concept of the highest good has fallen into disuse or seems at least to have become something secondary, hide the error (as they do many others) behind vague expressions; but one can nevertheless see this concept shine [65] through their systems since it always reveals heteronomy of practical reason, from which an a priori universally commanding moral law can never issue.

Now since the concepts of the good and evil, as consequences of the a priori determination of the will, presuppose also a pure practical principle and thus a causality of pure reason, they do not (as determinations of the synthetic unity of the manifold of given intuitions in one consciousness) refer originally to objects as do the pure concepts of the understanding or categories of the theoretically employed reason. Rather, they presuppose these objects as given, and they are without excep-

tion modes of a single category, that of causality, so far as its determining ground consists in reason's representation of a law
of causality which, as the law of freedom, reason gives itself,
thereby showing itself a priori to be practical. On the one side
the actions are under a law which is a law of freedom instead of
a natural law and thus belong to the conduct of intelligible
beings, and on the other side as events in the world of sense
they belong to appearances; so that the rules of practical reason
are possible only with respect to events in the world of sense
and consequently in accordance with the categories of the understanding. These rules, however, contribute nothing to the
theoretical use of the understanding in bringing the manifold
of (sensible) intuitions under one consciousness a priori, but
only to the a priori subjection of the *manifold of desires* to the
unity of consciousness of practical reason commanding in the
moral law, i.e., [to the consciousness] of a pure will.

These categories of freedom — for we wish to call them this
in contrast to the theoretical concepts which are categories of
nature — have a manifest advantage over the latter. The latter
categories are only forms of thought which, through universal
concepts, designate in an indefinite manner objects in general
for every intuition possible for us. The categories of freedom,
on the contrary, are elementary practical concepts which concern the decisions of the free faculty of choice; and though no
intuition perfectly corresponding to the latter can be given, the
categories of freedom have as their foundation a pure practical
law a priori, and this cannot be said for any of the concepts of
the theoretical use of our cognitive faculty. Instead of having as
its given basis the form of intuition (space and time), which
does not lie in reason itself but which rather has to be taken
over from sensibility, the elementary practical concepts [66]
have as their foundation *the form of a pure will given in reason*
and thus in the faculty of thought itself [and do not have to bor-
row their foundation from another faculty]. Since in all precepts of pure practical reason it is only a question of the decision of the will and not of the natural conditions (of practical
ability) for achieving its purpose, it thereby happens that the

practical concepts a priori in relation to the supreme principle of freedom immediately become cognitions, not needing to wait upon intuitions in order to acquire a meaning. This occurs for the noteworthy reason that they themselves produce the reality of that to which they refer (the disposition of the will) — an achievement which is in no way the business of theoretical concepts. One must carefully observe, however, that these categories concern only practical reason in general, and so they proceed in order from those which are as yet morally undetermined and sensuously conditioned to those which, being sensuously unconditioned, are determined only by the moral law.

TABLE OF THE CATEGORIES OF FREEDOM WITH REFERENCE TO THE CONCEPTS OF THE GOOD AND EVIL

1. Categories of Quantity
    Subjective, according to maxims (wishes and desires of the individual's will)
    Objective, according to principles (precepts)
    A priori principles of freedom, both subjective and objective (laws)
2. Categories of Quality
    Practical rules of commission (*praeceptivae*)
    Practical rules of omission (*prohibitivae*)
    Practical rules of exceptions (*exceptivae*)
3. Categories of Relation
    Relation to personality
    Relation to the condition [*Zustand*] of the person
    Reciprocally, relation of one person to the condition of others.
4. Categories of Modality
    The permitted and the forbidden
    Duty and that which is contrary to duty
    Perfect and imperfect duty

One quickly perceives that in this table freedom may [67] be regarded as a kind of causality (not subject to empirical grounds of determination) with reference to actions possible through freedom. These actions are regarded as appearances in

the world of sense, and consequently one sees that freedom re-
lates to the categories of the possibility of the actions in nature,
even though each category is taken in so universal a sense that
the determining ground of that causality can be assumed to lie
also beyond the world of sense in freedom as the property of an
intelligible being, until the categories of modality initiate the
transition, though only in a *problematical* way, from practical
principles in general to those of morality; and only later will it
be possible to establish the principles of moralilty in a *dogmatic* form through the moral law.

I add nothing here to elucidate the table, for it is sufficiently
understandable in itself. Such a division based on principles is
very useful in any science, for the sake of both thoroughness
and intelligibility. One knows immediately, for example, from
the table and its first division where one must begin in practical
considerations: with maxims which each person bases on his
inclinations, with precepts which hold for a species of rational
beings in so far as they agree in certain inclinations, and finally
with law, which holds for all irrespective of their inclinations.
And so on. In such a manner one surveys the whole plan of what
has to be done, every question of practical philosophy which
has to be answered, and also the order to be followed.

OF THE TYPIC OF THE PURE PRACTICAL
FACULTY OF JUDGMENT

The concepts of good and evil first determine an object for
the will. They themselves, however, stand under a practical
rule of reason which, if the reason is pure, determines the will a
priori in relation to its object. To decide whether an action
which is possible for us in the sensible world is or is not a case
under the rule requires the faculty of practical judgment, which
applies what is asserted universally in the rule (*in abstracto*) to
an action *in concreto*. A practical rule of pure reason, as *practical*, concerns the existence of an object, and, as practical *rule*
of pure reason, implies necessity with reference to the [68]
occurrence of an action; hence it is a practical law, not a natural

law because of empirical motives but a law of freedom by which the will is determinable independently of everything empirical and merely through the conception of a law in general and its form. Because of this, and since all instances of possible actions are only empirical and can belong only to experience and nature, it seems absurd to wish to find a case in the world of sense, and thus as a case always standing under the law of nature, which admits the application of a law of freedom to it and to which the supersensuous Idea could be applied so that the latter could be exhibited *in concreto*.

The faculty of judgment of pure practical reason, therefore, is subject to the same difficulties as that of the pure theoretical, though the latter had a means of escape. It could escape because in its theoretical use everything depended upon intuitions to which pure concepts of the understanding could be applied, and such intuitions can be given a priori (though only of objects of the senses), and, in what concerns the connection of the manifold in these intuitions, they can be given in a priori conformity with pure concepts of the understanding, i.e., as schemata. The morally good, on the contrary, is something which, with respect to its object, is supersensuous; nothing corresponding to it can be found in sensible intuition; consequently, judgment under laws of pure practical reason seems to be subject to special difficulties, which result from the fact that a law of freedom is to be applied to actions which are events occurring in the world of sense and thus, to this extent, belonging to nature.

But here again a favorable prospect for the faculty of pure practical judgment opens up. The subsumption under a pure practical law of an action which is possible to me in the world of sense does not concern the possibility of the action as an event in the world of sense. This possibility is a matter to be decided by the theoretical use of reason according to the law of causality, a pure concept of the understanding for which reason has a schema in sensible intuition. The physical causality or the condition under which it occurs belongs among the concepts of nature, whose schema is sketched by the transcendental imagination. Here, however, we are concerned not with the schema of a case occurring according to laws but with the schema (if this word is suitable here) of a law itself, because the determination of the will through law alone and without any other determining ground (and not the action with reference to [69] its consequences) connects the concept of causality to conditions altogether different from those which constitute connection in nature.

A schema is a universal procedure of imagination in presenting a priori to the senses the pure concept of the understanding which is determined by the law; and a schema must correspond to a natural law as a law to which objects of sensible intuition as such are subject. But to the law of freedom (which is a causality not sensuously conditioned), and consequently to the concept of the absolutely good, no intuition and hence no schema can be supplied for the purpose of applying it *in concreto*. Thus the moral law has no other cognitive faculty to mediate its application to objects of nature than the understanding (not the imagination); and the understanding can supply to an Idea of reason not a schema of sensibility but a law. This law, as one which can be exhibited *in concreto* in objects of the senses, is a natural law, but only in its form. This law can serve the purpose of the faculty of judgment, and it may, therefore, be called the *type* of the moral law.

The rule of the faculty of judgment under laws of pure practical reason is: Ask yourself whether, if the action which you propose should take place by a law of a nature of which you yourself were a part, you could regard it as possible through your will. Everyone does, in fact, decide by this rule whether actions are morally good or bad. Thus people ask: If one belonged to such an order of things that anyone would allow himself to deceive when he thought it to his advantage, or would feel justified in shortening his life as soon as he was thoroughly weary of it, or would look with complete indifference on the need of others, would he assent of his own will to being a member of such an order of things? Now everyone knows very well that if he secretly permits himself to deceive, it does not follow that everyone else will do so, or that if, unobserved by others, he is lacking in compassion, it does not mean that everyone else will immediately take the same attitude toward him. This comparison of the maxims of his actions with a universal natural law, therefore, is not the motive of his will. But such a law is still a type for the estimation of maxims according to moral principles. If the maxim of action is not so constituted as to stand the test of being made the form of a natural law in [70] general, it is morally impossible [though it may still be possible in nature]. Even common sense judges in this way, for its most ordinary judgments, even those of experience, are always based on natural law. Thus it is always at hand, but in cases where the causality from freedom is to be judged, natural law serves only as the *type* of a law of freedom, for if common sense did not have something to use in actual experience as an example, it could make no use of the law of pure practical reason in applying it to that experience.

We are therefore allowed to use nature, the sensible world, as the type of an intelligible nature, so long as we do not carry over to the latter intuitions and what depends on them but only apply to intelligible nature the form of lawfulness in general (the concept of which occurs in the most ordinary use of reason, though it cannot be known definitely a priori except with reference to the pure practical use of reason). For laws as such are all alike, regardless of whence they derive their determining grounds.

Furthermore, since of all intelligible objects absolutely nothing [is known] except freedom (through the moral law), and even this only in so far as it is a presupposition inseparable from the moral law; and since, moreover, all intelligible objects to which reason might eventually lead us under the guidance of the law can have no reality for us except for the purpose of this law and of the use of pure practical reason; and, finally, since reason has a right, and is even compelled, to use nature (in its pure intelligible form) as the type for the faculty of judgment — for all these reasons the present remark should serve to guard against counting among the concepts them-

selves what merely belongs to the typic of the concepts. This, as
the typic of the faculty judgment, guards against the empiricism
of practical reason, which bases the practical concepts of good
and evil merely on empirical consequences (on so-called happiness). Happiness and the infinite useful consequences of a
will determined only by [the maxim of] helping itself could
certainly, if this will made itself into a universal law of nature,
serve as a very adequate type for the morally good but still not
be identical with it.

The same typic guards also against the mysticism of practical
reason, which makes into a schema that which should serve
only as a symbol, i.e., proposes to supply real yet non- [71]
sensible intuitions (of an invisible kingdom of God) for the application of the moral law, and thus plunges into the transcendent. Only rationalism of the faculty of judgment is suitable to
the use of moral laws, for rationalism takes no more from sensible nature than that which pure reason can also think for itself,
i.e., lawfulness, and conversely transfers into the supersensible
nothing more than can be actually exhibited by actions in the
world of sense according to a formal rule of natural law in general. Thus the defense against empiricism of practical reason is
much more important and advisable, because mysticism is
compatible with the purity and sublimity of the moral law; and
as it is not natural to ordinary ways of thinking to stretch its
imagination to supersensible intuitions, the danger from this
side is not so general. On the other hand, empiricism uproots
the morality of dispositions, while the highest worth which
human beings can and should procure for themselves lies in
dispositions and not in actions only. It substitutes for duty
something entirely different, namely, an empirical interest,
with which inclinations generally are secretly in league. For
this reason empiricism is allied with the inclinations, which, no
matter what style they wear, always degrade humanity when
they are raised to the dignity of a supreme practical principle.
But these inclinations are so favorable to everyone's feelings
that empiricism is far more dangerous than all mystical enthusiasm, which can never be a lasting condition for any great number of people.

CHAPTER III

OF THE DRIVES OF PURE PRACTICAL REASON

What is essential in the moral worth of actions is that the moral law should directly determine the will. If the determination of the will occurs in accordance with the moral law but only by means of a feeling of any kind whatsoever, which must be presupposed in order that the law may become a determining ground of the will, and if the action does not occur for the sake of the law, it has legality but not morality. Now, if [72] by drive (*elater animi* [driver of the soul]) we understand a subjective determining ground of a will whose reason does not by its nature necessarily conform to the objective law, it follows, first, that absolutely no drives can be attributed to the Divine will; and, second, that the [moral] drive of the human will (and that of every created rational being) can never be anything other than the moral law; and, third, that the objective determining ground must at the same time be the exclusive and subjectively sufficient motive of action if the latter is to fulfil not merely the letter of the law but also its spirit.*

For the sake of the moral law and for the purpose of giving it influence on the will, one should not seek any other drive because of which the drive of the moral law itself might be dispensed with, producing only hypocrisy without any substance; it is risky even to let any other drives (such as [a desire for] advantage) collaborate with the moral law. Thus there remains nothing to do except to determine in what way the moral law becomes the drive, and to see what happens to the human faculty of desire as a consequence of this motive. For how a law in itself can be the direct motive of the will (which is the essence of morality) is an insoluble problem for the human reason. It is identical with the problem of how a free will is possible. Therefore, we shall not have to show a priori the source from which

---

*Of every action which conforms to the law but does not occur for the sake of the law, one may say that it is morally good in letter but not in spirit (in disposition).

the moral law supplies a drive but rather what it effects (or better, must effect) in the mind, so far as it is a drive.

The essential point in all determination of the will through the moral law is this: as a free will, and thus not only without co-operating with sensuous impulses but even rejecting all of them and checking all inclinations so far as they could be antagonistic to the law, it is determined merely by the law. Thus far, the effect of the moral law as a drive is only negative, and as such this drive can be known a priori. For all inclination and every sensuous impulse is based on feeling, and the [73] negative effect on feeling (through the check on the inclinations) is itself feeling. Consequently, we can see a priori that the moral law as a ground of determination of the will, by thwarting all our inclinations, must produce a feeling which can be called pain. Here we have the first and perhaps the only case wherein we can determine from a priori concepts the relation of a cognition (here a cognition of pure practical reason) to the feeling of pleasure or displeasure. All inclinations taken together (which can be brought into a fairly tolerable system, whereupon their satisfaction is called happiness) constitute self-regard (*solipsismus*). This consists either of self-love, which is a predominant benevolence toward one's self (*philautia*) or of self-satisfaction (*arrogantia*). The former is called, more particularly, selfishness; the latter, self-conceit. Pure practical reason merely checks selfishness, for selfishness, natural and active in us even prior to the moral law, is restricted by the moral law to agreement with the law; when this is done, selfishness is called rational self-love. But it strikes self-conceit down, since all claims of self-esteem which precede conformity to the moral law are null and void. For the certainty of a disposition which agrees with this law is the first condition of any worth of the person (as will soon be made clear), and any presumption [to worth] prior to this is false and opposed to the law. Now the propensity to self-esteem, so long as it rests only on the sensuous, is one of the inclinations which the moral law checks. Therefore, the moral law strikes down self-conceit.

Since this law, however, is in itself positive, being the form of an intellectual causality, i.e., the form of freedom, it is at the same time an object of respect, since, in conflict with its subjective antagonists (our inclinations), it weakens self-conceit. And as striking down, i.e., humiliating, self-conceit, it is an object of the greatest respect and thus the ground of a positive feeling which is not of empirical origin. This feeling, then, is one which can be known a priori. Respect for the moral law, therefore, is a feeling produced by an intellectual cause, and this feeling is the only one which we can know completely a priori and the necessity of which we can discern.

In the preceding chapter we have seen that any- [74] thing which presents itself as the object of the will prior to the moral law is excluded from the motives of the will (which is called unconditionally good) by the law itself as the supreme condition of practical reason. We have also seen that the mere practical form, which consists in the competency of the maxims to give universal laws, first determines what is of itself and absolutely good and is the ground of the maxims of a pure will, which alone is good in every respect. We find now, however, our nature as sensuous beings so characterized that the material of the faculty of desire (objects of the inclination, whether of hope or fear) first presses upon us; and we find our pathologically determinable self, although by its maxims it is wholly incapable of giving universal laws, striving to give its pretensions priority and to make them acceptable as first and original claims, just as if our pathologically determined self were our entire self. This propensity to make the subjective motives of one's choice into an objective motive of the will in general can be called self-love; when it makes itself legislative and an unconditional practical principle, it can be called self-conceit. The moral law, which alone is truly, i.e., in every respect, objective, completely excludes the influence of self-love from the highest practical principle and forever checks self-conceit, which decrees the subjective conditions of self-love as laws. If anything checks our self-conceit in our own judgment, it humiliates. Therefore, the moral law inevitably humbles every man when he compares the sensuous propensity of his nature with the law. Now if the idea of something as the motive of the will humiliates us in our self-consciousness, it awakens respect for itself so far as it is a positive motive. The moral law, therefore, is even subjectively a cause of respect.

Now everything in self-love belongs to inclination, and all inclination rests on feelings; therefore, whatever checks all inclinations in self-love necessarily has, by that fact, an influence on feeling. Thus we conceive how it is possible to understand a priori that the moral law can exercise an effect on feeling, since it blocks the inclinations and the propensity to make them the supreme practical condition (i.e., self-love) in the enunciation of supreme law. This effect is on the one side merely negative; but on the other, in respect to the restrictive practical [75] ground of pure practical reason, it is positive. And to the latter, no kind of feeling, [even] under the name of a practical or moral feeling, may be assumed as prior to the moral law and as its basis.

The negative effect on feeling (unpleasantness) is, like all influence on feeling and every feeling itself, pathological.[1] As the effect of the consciousness of the moral law, and consequently in relation to an intelligible cause, i.e., to the subject of the pure practical reason as the supreme legislator, this feeling of a rational subject affected with inclinations is called humiliation (intellectual contempt). But in relation to its positive ground, the law, it is at the same time respect for the law; for this law there is no feeling, but, as it removes a resistance, this dislodgment of an obstacle is, in the judgment of reason, equally esteemed as a positive assistance to its causality. Therefore, this feeling can also be called a feeling of respect for the moral law; on both grounds, it can be called a moral feeling.

Thus the moral law, as formal determining ground of action through practical pure reason, and moreover as a material

[1]By *pathological* Kant did not mean diseased or abnormal; *pathological* pertained to the emotions and passions.

though purely objective determining ground of the objects of
action (under the name of good and evil), is also a subjective
motive. That is, it is the drive to this action, since it has an influence on the sensuousness of the subject and effects a feeling
which promotes the influence of the law on the will. In the
subject there is no *antecedent feeling* tending to morality;
that is impossible, because all feeling is sensuous, and the
drives of the moral disposition must be free from every sensuous condition. Rather, sensuous feeling, which is the basis of
all our inclinations, is the condition of the particular feeling we
call respect, but the cause that determines this feeling lies in
pure practical reason; because of its origin, therefore, this particular feeling cannot be said to be pathologically effected;
rather, it is practically effected. Since the idea of the moral law
deprives self-love of its influence and self-conceit of its delusion, it lessens the obstacle to pure practical reason and produces the idea of the superiority of its objective law to [76]
the impulses of sensuousness; it increases the weight of the
moral law by removing, in the judgment of reason, the counter-
weight to the moral law which bears on a will affected by the
sensuous. Thus respect for the law is not the drive to morality; it
is morality itself, regarded subjectively as a drive, inasmuch as
pure practical reason, by rejecting all the rival claims of self-
love, gives authority and absolute sovereignty to the law. It
should be noticed that, as respect is an effect on feeling and
thus on the sensuousness of a rational being, it presupposes the
sensuousness and hence the finitude of such beings on whom
respect for the moral law is imposed; thus respect for the law
cannot be attributed to a supreme being or even to one free
from all sensuousness, since in such a being there could be no
obstacle to practical reason.

   This feeling, under the name of moral feeling, is therefore
produced solely by reason. It does not serve in estimating actions or as a basis of the objective moral law itself but only as a
drive to make this law itself its maxim. By what name better
than moral feeling could we call this singular feeling, which
cannot be compared with any pathological feeling? It is of such

a peculiar kind that it seems to be at the disposal only of reason, and indeed only of pure practical reason.

Respect always applies to persons only, never to things. The latter can awaken inclinations, and even love if they are animals (horses, dogs, etc.), or fear, as does the sea, a volcano, or a beast of prey; but they never arouse respect. Something which approaches this feeling is admiration, and this, as an emotion (wonder) can refer also to things, e.g., lofty mountains, the magnitude, number, and distance of the heavenly bodies, the strength and swiftness of many animals, etc. None of this, however, is respect. A man can also be an object of love, fear, or admiration even to wonderment, and yet not be an object of respect. His jocular humor, his courage and strength, and his power of rank may inspire me with such feelings, though inner respect for him is still lacking. Fontenelle[2] says, "I bow to a great man, but my mind does not bow." I can add: to a [77] humble plain man, in whom I perceive righteousness in a higher degree than I am conscious of in myself, *my mind bows* whether I choose or not, however high I carry my head that he may not forget my superior position. Why? His example holds a law before me which strikes down my self-conceit when I compare my own conduct with it; that it is a law which can be obeyed, and consequently is one that can actually be put into practice, is proved to my eyes by the act. I may even be conscious of a like degree of righteousness in myself, and yet respect remains. In men all good is defective, but the law made visible in an example always humbles my pride, since the man whom I see before me provides me with a standard by clearly appearing to me in a more favorable light in spite of his imperfections, which, though perhaps always with him, are not so well known to me as are my own. Respect is a tribute we cannot refuse to pay to merit whether we will or not; we can indeed outwardly withhold it, but we cannot help feeling it inwardly.

---

[2]Bernard Le Bovier de Fontenelle (1657–1757), a French popular philosopher.

Respect is so far from being a feeling of pleasure that one only reluctantly gives way to it when it is respect for a man. We seek to discover something in him that will lighten the burden of it for us, some fault in him to compensate us for the humiliation which we suffer from such an example. The dead themselves are not immune from this criticism, especially when their example appears inimitable. Even the moral law itself in its solemn majesty is exposed to this endeavor to keep one's self from yielding respect to it. Can it be thought that there is any reason why we like to degrade it to the level of our familiar inclination and why we take so much trouble to make it the chosen precept of our well-understood interest, other than the fact that we want to be free of the awesome respect which so severely shows us our own unworthiness? Nevertheless, there is on the other hand so little displeasure in it that, when once we renounce our self-conceit and respect has established its practical influence, we cannot ever satisfy ourselves in contemplating the majesty of this law, and the soul believes itself to be elevated in proportion as it sees the holy law as elevated over it and its frail nature.

Certainly, great talents and activity proportionate to them can occasion respect or an analogous feeling, and it is [78] proper to accord it to them; then it seems that admiration is the same as this feeling [of respect]. But if one looks more closely it is noticed that it is always uncertain how great a part of the ability we admire must be ascribed to innate talent and how much to cultivation through the person's own diligence. Presumably reason represents it to us as a fruit of cultivation, and therefore as merit which perceptibly diminishes our self-conceit and therefore either reproaches us or imposes it upon us as an example to be followed. This respect which we have for a person (really for the law, which his example holds before us) is, therefore, not mere admiration. This is also confirmed by the way the common run of men give up their respect for a man (e.g., Voltaire) when they think they have in some manner found the badness of his character, while the true scholar still feels this respect at least for his talents, since he is himself involved in an activity and vocation which makes imitation of him to some extent a law.

Respect for the moral law is therefore the sole and undoubted moral drive, and this feeling is directed to no being except on this basis. First, the moral law determines the will directly and objectively in the judgment of reason. Freedom, the causality of which is determinable only through the law, consists, however, only in the fact that it limits all inclinations, including self-esteem, to the condition of obedience to its pure law. This limitation exerts an effect on feeling and produces the sensation of displeasure, which can be known a priori from the moral law. Since, however, it is so far a merely negative effect originating from the influence of pure practical reason, it checks the activity of the subject to the extent that inclinations are its motives, and consequently it checks also the pretensions to personal worth, which is nothing without accordance with the moral law. Thus the effect of this law on feeling is humiliation alone, which we thus see a priori, though we cannot know the force of the pure practical law as drive but only the resistance to the drives of our sensuous nature. This same law, [79] however, is objectively, i.e., in the conception of pure reason, a direct determining ground of the will. Hence this humiliation occurs proportionately to the purity of the law; for that reason the lowering (humiliation) of the pretensions to moral self-esteem on the sensuous side is an elevation of the moral, i.e., practical, esteem for the law on the intellectual side. In a word, respect for the law is thus by virtue of its intellectual cause a positive feeling that can be known a priori, for any diminution of obstacles to an activity furthers this activity itself. The acknowledgment of the moral law is the consciousness of an activity of practical reason on objective grounds, and it fails to express its effect in actions simply because subjective (pathological) causes hinder it. Therefore, respect for the moral law must be regarded also as a positive but indirect effect of the law on feeling, in so far as the law weakens the hindering influence of the inclinations through humiliating self-conceit; consequently, we must see it as a subjective motive of activity, as a drive to obey the law and as the ground of maxims of a course of life conformable to the law.

From the concept of drive there comes that of an interest, which can never be attributed to a being which lacks reason; it indicates a drive of the will so far as it is presented by reason. Since the law itself must be the drive in a morally good will, the moral interest must be a pure nonsensuous interest of practical reason alone. Now on the concept of an interest rests that of a maxim. A maxim is thus morally genuine only when it rests on exclusive interest in obedience to the law. All three concepts — of drive, interest, and maxim — can, however, be applied only to finite beings. For without exception they presuppose a limitation of the nature of the being, in that the subjective character of its choice does not of itself agree with the objective law of practical reason; they presuppose that the being must be impelled in some manner to action, since an internal obstacle stands against it. They cannot, therefore, be applied to the divine will.

In the boundless esteem for the pure moral law, removed from all advantage, as practical reason presents it to us for [80] obedience, whose voice makes even the boldest sinner tremble and forces him to hide himself from it, there is something so singular that we cannot wonder at finding this influence of a merely intellectual Idea on feeling to be inexplicable to speculative reason, and at having to be satisfied with being able to see a priori that such a feeling is inseparably bound with the Idea of the moral law in every finite rational being. If this feeling of respect were pathological and thus a feeling of pleasure grounded on the inner sense, it would be futile to try to discover a relation of the feeling to any representation a priori. But it is a feeling which is concerned only with the practical, and with the representation of a law simply as to its form and not on account of any object of the law; thus it cannot be reckoned either as enjoyment or as pain, yet it produces an interest in obedience to the law, and this we call *moral interest*. And the capacity of taking such an interest in the law (or of having respect for the moral law itself) is really moral feeling.

The consciousness of free submission of the will to the law, combined with an inevitable constraint imposed only by our own reason on all inclinations, is respect for the law. The law which commands and inspires this respect is, as we see, no other than the moral law, for no other law precludes all inclinations from having a direct influence on the will. The action which is objectively practical according to this law and excludes inclination from its determining grounds is called *duty*; and, because of this exclusion, in the concept of duty there is that of practical constraint, i.e., determination to actions however reluctantly they may be done. The feeling which arises from the consciousness of this constraint is not pathological, as are those caused by objects of the senses, but practical, i.e., possible through prior (objective) determination of the will and causality of reason. As submission to a law, i.e., as a command which constrains the sensuously affected subject, it contains, therefore, no pleasure but rather displeasure proportionate to this constraint. On the other hand, since this constraint is exercised only through the legislation of one's own reason, it also contains something elevating, and the subjective effect on feeling, in so far as pure practical reason is its sole cause, [81] can also be called self-approbation with reference to pure practical reason, for one knows himself to be determined thereto solely by the law and without any [sensuous] interest; he becomes conscious of an altogether different interest which is subjectively produced by the law and which is purely practical and free. Our taking this interest in a dutiful action is not prompted by inclination, but the practical law absolutely commands it and also actually produces it. Consequently, it has a very special name, viz., respect.

The concept of duty thus requires of action that it objectively agree with the law, while of the maxim of the action it demands subjective respect for the law as the sole mode of determining the will through itself. And thereon rests the distinction between consciousness of having acted *according to duty* and *from duty*, i.e., from respect for the law. The former, legality, is possible even if inclinations alone are the determining grounds of the will, but the latter, morality or moral worth, can be conceded only where the action occurs from duty, i.e., merely for the sake of the law.*

It is of the utmost importance in all moral judging to pay strictest attention to the subjective principle of every maxim, so that all the morality of actions may be placed in their necessity from duty and from respect for the law, and not from love for or leaning toward that which the action is to produce. For men and all rational creatures, the moral necessity is a constraint, an obligation. Every action based on it is to be considered as duty, and not as a manner of acting which we naturally favor or which we sometime might favor. This would be tantamount to believing we could finally bring it about that, without respect for the law (which is always connected with fear or at least [82] apprehension that we might transgress it) we, like the independent deity, might come into possession of holiness of will through irrefragable agreement of the will with the pure moral law becoming, as it were, our very nature. This pure law, if we could never be tempted to be untrue to it, would finally cease altogether to be a command for us.

The moral law is, in fact, for the will of a perfect being a law of holiness. For the will of any finite rational being, however, it is a law of duty, of moral constraint, and of the determination of his actions through respect for the law and reverence for his duty. No other subjective principle must be assumed as the drive, for though it might happen that the action occurs as the law prescribes, and thus in accord with duty but not from duty, the disposition to do the action would not be moral, and it is the disposition which is precisely in question in this legislation.

---

*If one examines more accurately the concept of respect for persons, as this has been previously presented, one will perceive that it always rests on the consciousness of a duty which an example holds before us, and that consequently respect can never have other than a moral ground. It is also seen to be very good and, from the psychological point of view, very useful to our understanding of human nature, that wherever we use the term to pay attention to the mysterious and wonderful, but frequent, regard which human judgment does have for the moral law.

It is a very beautiful thing to do good to human beings because of love and a sympathetic good will, or to do justice because of a love of order. But this is not yet the genuine moral
maxim of conduct, the maxim befitting our position among rational beings as men, when we presume, like volunteers, to
flout with proud conceit the thought of duty and, as independent of command, merely to will of our own good pleasure to
do something to which we think we need no command. We
stand under a *discipline* of reason, and in all our maxims we
must not forget our subjection to it, or withdraw anything from
it, or by an egotistical illusion detract from the authority of the
law (even though it is one given by our own reason), so that we
could place the motive of our will (even though it is in accordance with the law) elsewhere than in the law itself and in respect for it. Duty and obligation are the only names which we
must give to our relation to the moral law. We are indeed legislative members of a moral realm which is possible through
freedom and which is presented to us as an object of respect by
practical reason; yet we are at the same time subjects in it, not
sovereigns, and to mistake our inferior position as creatures
and to deny, from self-conceit, respect to the holy law is, in [83]
spirit, a defection from it even if its letter be fulfilled.

The possibility of such a command as, "Love God above all
and thy neighbor as thyself,"* agrees very well with this. For, as
a command, it requires esteem for a law which orders love and
does not leave it to arbitrary choice to make love the principle.
But love to God as inclination (pathological love) is impossible, for He is not an object of the senses. The latter is indeed
possible toward men, but it cannot be commanded, for it is not
possible for a person to love someone merely on command. It
is, therefore, only practical love which can be understood in
that kernel of all laws. To love God means in this sense to do

*The principle of one's own happiness, which some wish to make the su-
preme principle of morality, is in striking contrast to this law. This principle
would read: "Love thyself above all, but God and thy neighbor for thine own
sake."

His commandments gladly, and to love one's neighbor means to practice all duties toward him gladly. The command which makes this a rule cannot require that we have this disposition but only that we endeavor after it. To command that one do something gladly is self-contradictory. For a law would not be needed if we already knew of ourselves what we ought to do and moreover were conscious of liking to do it; and if we did it without liking but only out of respect for the law, a command which makes just this respect the drive of the maxim would counteract the disposition it commands. That law of all laws, like every moral prescription of the Gospel, thus presents the moral disposition in its complete perfection, and though as an ideal of holiness it is unattainable by any creature, it is yet an archetype which we should strive to approach and to imitate in an uninterrupted infinite progress. If a rational creature could ever reach the stage of thoroughly liking to do all that moral laws require, it would mean that there was no possibility of there being in him a desire which could tempt him to deviate from them, for overcoming such a desire always costs the subject some sacrifice and requires self-compulsion, i.e., an inner constraint to do that which one does not quite like to do. To such a level of moral disposition no creature can ever [84] attain. For since he is a creature, and consequently is always dependent with respect to what he needs for complete satisfaction with his condition, he can never be wholly free from desires and inclinations which, because they rest on physical causes, do not of themselves agree with the moral law, which has an entirely different source. Consequently, with reference to these desires it is always necessary to base the disposition of the creature's maxims on moral constraint and not on ready willingness, i.e., to base it on respect which demands obedience to the law even though the creature does not like to do it, and not on love, which apprehends no inward reluctance of the will to obey the law. This would be true even if mere love for the law (which would in this case cease to be a command, and morality, subjectively passing over into holiness, would cease to be virtue) were made the constant but unattainable goal of its striving. For in the case of what we esteem and yet dread because of our consciousness of our weaknesses, the most reverential awe would be changed into inclination, and respect into love, because of the greater ease in satisfying the latter. At least this would be the perfection of a disposition dedicated to the law, if it were ever possible for a creature to attain it.

This reflection is not intended so much to clarify by exact concepts the Gospel command just cited in order to prevent religious fanaticism with reference to the love of God as to define accurately the moral disposition directly with regard to our duties to others and to control and, if possible, to prevent a narrow moral fanaticism, which infects many persons. The stage of morality on which man (and, so far as we know, every rational creature) stands is respect for moral law. The disposition which obliges him to obey it is: to obey it from duty and not from a spontaneous inclination or from an endeavor unbidden but gladly undertaken. The moral condition which he can always be in is virtue, i.e., moral disposition in conflict, and not holiness in the supposed possession of perfect purity of the dispositions of will. By exhortation to actions as noble, sublime, and magnanimous, the mind is disposed to nothing but blatant moral fanaticism and exaggerated self-conceit. By [85] such exhortation people are led into the illusion that the motive [of their moral actions] is not duty (i.e., respect for the law) whose yoke they must reluctantly bear even though it is a mild yoke imposed by reason. This law always humbles them when they follow (obey) it, but by this kind of exhortation they come to think that those actions are expected of them not because of duty but only because of their own bare merit. For not only do they not fulfil the spirit of the law when they imitate such acts on the basis of such a principle, since the spirit of the law lies in the submissive disposition and not in the merely lawful character of the act, leaving the principle to be what it may; and not only do they in this manner make the drives pathological (locating them in sympathy or self-love) and not moral (located in the law); but they produce in this way a shallow, high-flown, fantastic way of thinking, flattering themselves with a spontaneous goodness of heart, needing neither spur nor bridle nor even command, and thereby forgetting their obligation, which they ought to think of rather than their merit. Certainly actions of others which have been done with great sacrifice and solely for the sake of duty may be praised as noble and sublime deeds, yet only in so far as there are clues which suggest that they were done wholly out of respect for duty and not from aroused feelings. But if anyone wishes to put them forward as examples for imitation, the drive to be employed must be only respect for duty, the sole genuine moral feeling, this earnest holy precept which does not leave it to our vain self-love to dally with pathological impulses (as far as they are analogous to morality) and to pride ourselves on our meritorious worth. For all actions which are praiseworthy, if we only search we shall find a law of duty which commands and does not leave us to choose what may be agreeable to our propensity. That is the only way of representing [morality] which morally educates the soul, because it is the only one which is capable of firm and accurately defined principles.

If fanaticism in its most general sense is a deliberate overstepping of the boundaries of human reason, moral fanaticism is this overstepping of boundaries which practical pure reason sets to mankind. Pure practical reason thereby forbids us [86] to place the subjective motive of dutiful actions, i.e., their moral incentive, anywhere else than in the law itself, and to place the disposition which is thereby brought into the maxims elsewhere than in the respect for this law; it commands that we make the thought of duty, which strikes down all arrogance as well as vain self-love, the supreme life-principle of all human morality.

If this is so, then not only novelists and sentimental educators (even though they may be zealously opposed to sentimentalism) but also philosophers and indeed the strictest of them, the Stoics, have instituted moral fanaticism instead of a sober but wise moral discipline, though the fanaticism of the latter was more heroic, while that of the former is of a more shallow and pliable nature. And we may, without hypocrisy, truly say of the moral teaching of the Gospel that, through the purity of its moral principle and at the same time through the suitability of its principle to the limitations of finite beings, it first brought all good conduct of man under the discipline of duty clearly set before him, which does not permit him to indulge in fancies of moral perfections; and that it set limits of humility (i.e., self-knowledge) on self-conceit as well as on self-love, both of which readily mistake their boundaries.

Duty! Thou sublime and mighty name that dost embrace nothing charming or insinuating but requirest submission and yet seekest not to move the will by threatening aught that would arouse natural aversion or terror, but only holdest forth a law which of itself finds entrance into the mind and yet gains reluctant reverence (though not always obedience) — a law before which all inclinations are mute even though they secretly work against it: what origin is worthy of thee, and where is the root of thy noble descent which proudly rejects all kinship with the inclinations and from which to be descended is the indispensable condition of the only worth which men alone can give themselves?

This root cannot be less than something that elevates man above himself as a part of the world of sense, something which connects him with an order of things which only the understanding can think and which has under it the entire world of sense, including the empirically determinable existence of man in time, and the whole system of all ends which is [87] alone suitable to such unconditional practical laws as the moral. It is nothing else than *personality*, i.e., the freedom and independence from the mechanism of nature regarded as a capacity of a being subject to special laws (pure practical laws given by its own reason), so that the person belonging to the world of sense is subject to his own personality so far as he belongs to the intelligible world. For it is then not to be wondered at that man, as belonging to two worlds, must regard his own being in relation to his second and higher vocation with reverence, and the laws of this vocation with the deepest respect.

Many expressions which indicate the worth of objects according to moral ideas have this origin. The moral law is holy (inviolable). Man is certainly unholy enough, but humanity in his person must be holy to him. Everything in creation which he wishes and over which he has power can be used merely as a means; only man, and, with him, every rational creature, is an end in himself. He is the subject of the moral law which is holy, because of the autonomy of his freedom. Because of the latter, every will, even the private will of each person directed to himself, is restricted to the condition of agreement with the autonomy of the rational being, namely, that it should be directed to no purpose which would not be possible by a law which could issue from the will of the subject who is the passive recipient of the action. This condition thus requires that the person never be used as a means except when he is at the same time treated as an end. We may rightly attribute this condition even to the divine will with respect to the rational beings in the world as its creatures, since the condition rests on the personality of these beings, whereby alone they are ends in themselves.

This idea of personality awakens respect; it places before our eyes the sublimity of our own nature (in its [higher] vocation), while it shows us at the same time the unsuitability of our conduct to it, thus striking down our self-conceit. This is naturally and easily observed by the most common human reason. Has not every even fairly honest man sometimes found that he desists from an otherwise harmless lie which would extricate him from a vexing affair or which would even be useful to a [88] beloved and deserving friend simply in order not to have to shame himself secretly in his own eyes? In the greatest misfortunes of his life which he could have avoided if he could have disregarded duty, does not a righteous man hold up his head thanks to the consciousness that he has honored and preserved humanity in his own person and in its dignity, so that he does not have to shame himself in his own eyes or have reason to fear the inner scrutiny of self-examination? This comfort is not happiness, not even the smallest part of happiness; for no one would wish to have occasion for it, not even once in his life, or perhaps would even desire life itself in such circumstances. But he lives and cannot tolerate seeing himself as unworthy of life. This inner satisfaction is therefore merely negative with reference to everything which might make life pleasant; it is the defense against the danger of sinking in personal worth after the value of his circumstances has been completely lost. It is the effect of a respect for something entirely different from life, in comparison and contrast to which life and its enjoyment have absolutely no worth. He yet lives only because it is his duty, not because he has the least taste for living.

Such is the nature of the genuine drive of pure practical reason. It is nothing else than the pure moral law itself, so far as it lets us perceive the sublimity of our own supersensuous existence and subjectively effects respect for the higher vocation in men who are conscious of their sensuous existence and of the accompanying dependence on their pathologically affected nature. Now let there be associated with this drive so many charms and pleasures of life that even for their sake alone the most skillful choice of a reasonable Epicurean, considering the highest welfare of life, would declare himself for moral conduct (and it may even be advisable to connect this prospect of a gladsome enjoyment of life with that supreme determining motive which is sufficient of itself); but this is only in order to hold a balance against the attractions which vice on the other side does not fail to offer and not in order to place in these prospects even the smallest part of the real moving force when duty is what we are concerned with. For the latter would simply destroy the purity of the moral disposition at its source. The majesty of duty has nothing to do with the enjoyment of life; [89] it has its own law, even its own tribunal, and however much one wishes to shake them together, in order to offer the mixture to the sick soul as though it were a medicine, they nevertheless soon separate of themselves; but, if they do not separate, the moral ingredient has no effect at all, and even if the physical life gained some strength in this way, the moral life would waste away beyond recovery.

CRITICAL ELUCIDATION OF THE ANALYTIC OF
PURE PRACTICAL REASON

By a critical elucidation of a science or of one of its portions that is a system by itself, I understand the investigation and jus- tification of the fact that it must have precisely the systematic form which it does have and no other when compared with an- other system which has as its basis a similar cognitive faculty. Now practical reason has the same cognitive faculty for its foundation as the speculative, so far as they are both pure rea- son. Thus the difference in their systematic form must be de- termined by a comparison between them, and the ground of this difference be given.

The Analytic of pure theoretical reason deals with knowl- edge of objects which may be given to the understanding. It therefore had to begin from intuition and consequently (since intuition is always sensible) from sensibility; only then could it progress to concepts (of objects of this intuition); it could end with principles only after these two had been dealt with. On the other hand, practical reason is concerned not with objects in order to know them but with its own capacity to make them real (which does require knowledge of them), i.e., it has to do with a will which is a causal agent so far as reason contains its deter- mining ground. Consequently, it does not have to furnish an object of intuition, but as practical reason it has only to give a law [for objects] of intuition, because the concept of causality always contains a relation to a law which determines the exis- tence of the many in their relation to one another. Thus a cri- tique of the Analytic of reason, if it is to be practical reason (which is the real problem), must begin from the possibility of practical fundamental principles a priori. Only from [90] these can it proceed to concepts of objects of a practical reason, i.e., to the concepts of the absolutely good and evil in order first to assign them in accordance with those principles, for prior to those principles there is no cognitive faculty by which they could be given as good and evil. Only then could the last chapter, dealing with the relation of pure practical reason to the sensuous and with its necessary influence on it, i.e., the moral feeling which is known a priori, close this part of the work. Thus the Analytic of practical pure reason distinguishes among the conditions of its use in a way analogous to that of the theoretical reason but in reverse order.[3] The Analytic of theoretical pure reason was divided into Transcendental Aesthetic and Transcendental Logic; that of practical reason is divided, conversely, into Logic and Aesthetic of pure practical reason, if I may be allowed to use, on the basis of analogy, these terms which are not entirely suitable. The Logic in turn was there divided into Analytic of Concepts and Analytic of Principles; here it is divided into that of principles and concepts. The Aesthetic had there two parts, because of the dual nature of sensible intuition; here the sensibility is regarded not as a faculty of intuition but merely as feeling (which can be a subjective ground of desire), and in this respect pure practical reason allows no further subdivision.

The reason this division into two parts together with their subdivision is not actually carried out is easily seen, even though in the beginning an attempt to do this might have been tempting because of the example of the first *Critique*. For since it is pure reason, which is here seen in its practical use and thus as commencing from a priori principles and not from empirical motives, the division of the Analytic of Pure Practical Reason

---

[3]The analogy drawn is erroneous. The *Critique of Pure Reason* is actually divided as follows:

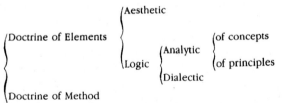

For a simpler statement of the relationship between the organization of the two *Critiques*, see above, p. 16.

must turn out to be similar to that of a syllogism, i.e., proceeding from the universal in the major premise (the moral principle), through a minor premise containing a subsumption of possible actions (as good or evil) under the major, to the conclusion, viz., the subjective determination of the will (an interest in the practically possible good and the maxim based on it). Whoever has been able to convince himself of the truth of the propositions in the Analytic will get a certain enjoyment out of such comparisons, for they correctly occasion the [91] expectation of bringing some day into one view the unity of the entire pure rational faculty (both theoretical and practical) and of being able to derive everything from one principle. The latter is an unavoidable need of human reason, as it finds complete satisfaction only in a perfectly systematic unity of its cognitions.

But if we regard also the content of the knowledge which we can have of and through pure practical reason, as the Analytic presents this content, there is to be found, besides a remarkable analogy between it and the content of theoretical knowledge, no less remarkable differences. With reference to the theoretical, the faculty of pure rational a priori knowledge could be easily and obviously proved through examples from the sciences (in which one does not need so much to fear a secret admixture of empirical grounds of cognition as in ordinary knowledge, since the sciences put their principles to the test in so many ways by methodical use). But that pure reason is of itself alone practical, without any admixture of any kind of empirical motives—one had to show this from the commonest practical use of reason by producing evidence that the highest practical principle is a principle recognized by every natural human reason as the supreme law of its will, as a law completely a priori and independent of any sensuous data. It was necessary first to establish and justify it, by proof of the purity of its origin, in the judgment of common reason, before science could take it in hand to make use of it, so to speak, as a fact which precedes all disputation about its possibility and all consequences which may be drawn from it. But this circumstance is easily explained from what has previously been said: it is be-

cause practical pure reason necessarily must begin with fundamental principles, which thus, as the original data, must be
made the basis of the whole science and not regarded as first
originating from it. On this account, the justification of moral
principles as principles of pure reason could be made with sufficient certainty through merely appealing to the judgment of
common sense, since everything empirical which might insin-
uate itself into our maxims as a motive of the will immediately reveals itself through the feeling of enjoyment or [92]
pain which necessarily attaches to it in so far as it arouses desire, and pure practical reason immediately refuses to take it as
a condition into its principle. The dissimilarity of rational and
empirical motives is made recognizable through the resistance
of a practically legislating reason to all interfering inclinations,
which is shown in a peculiar kind of feeling which does not
precede the legislation of practical reason but which is, on the
contrary, first effected by it, as a compulsion. That is, it is revealed through the feeling of respect of a kind that no man has
for any inclinations whatever, but which he may feel for the law
alone. It is shown so saliently and prominently that no one, not
even the commonest mind, can fail in a moment to discover in
an example that, though he can be urged by empirical grounds
of volition to follow their attractions, he can be expected to
obey nothing but the pure practical law of reason.

In the doctrine of happiness empirical principles constitute
the entire foundation, but in the doctrine of morality they do
not form even the smallest part of it. The differentiation between these two is the first and most important task charged to
the Analytic of Pure Practical Reason, and in it we must proceed
as exactly and as punctiliously as ever a geometer went about
his job. But the philosopher here (as everywhere else in rational knowledge, having to use mere concepts without any constructions for them) must struggle with greater difficulties than
the geometer, because he can take no intuition ([of] a pure
noumenon) as a foundation. He has the advantage, however,
that, almost like the chemist, he can at any time arrange an ex-
periment with the practical reason of any man, in order to dis-

tinguish the moral (pure) motive from the empirical; he does
so when he adds the moral law (as a motive) to the empirically
affected will (e.g., to the will of a person who would like to tell
a lie so that he could thereby gain something). When the ana-
lyst adds alkali to a solution of calcareous earth in muriatic acid,
the acid releases the lime and combines with the alkali, and the
lime precipitates. Just in the same way, if a man who is otherwise honest (or who this one time puts himself only in thought
in the place of an honest man) is confronted with the moral
law, by which he recognizes the worthlessness of the [93]
liar, his practical reason, in its judgment of what ought to be
done, immediately forsakes the advantage and combines with
that which maintains in him his respect for his own person
(truthfulness), and the advantage is easily weighed by anyone
after it is separated and washed of every particle of reason
(which is wholly on the side of duty), so that it can enter into
combination with reason in still other cases, though not in any
case where it could be opposed to the moral law, for reason
never forsakes this but rather combines most closely with it.

But this distinction of the principle of happiness from that of
morality is not for this reason an opposition between them, and
pure practical reason does not require that we should renounce
the claims to happiness; it requires only that we take no account of them whenever duty is in question. It can even be a
duty in certain respects to provide for one's happiness, in part
because (since it includes skill, health, and riches) it contains
means to the fulfilment of one's duty and in part because the
lack of it (e.g., poverty) contains temptations to transgress
against duty. But to further one's happiness can never be a direct duty, and even less can it be a principle of all duty. Since all
motives of the will (except the one and only pure practical law
of reason, i.e., the moral law) are empirical and as such belong
to the principle of happiness, they must be separated from the
supreme practical principle and never be incorporated with it
as a condition, for this would destroy all moral worth just as
surely as any admixture of anything empirical in geometrical
axioms would destroy all mathematical certainty, which is, ac-

cording to Plato's judgment, the highest excellence mathematics has, surpassing even its utility.

But instead of the deduction of the supreme principle of pure practical reason, i.e., the explanation of the possibility of such a cognition a priori, nothing more could be done than to show that, if we saw the possibility of freedom of an efficient cause, we would see not only the possibility but also the necessity of the moral law as the supreme practical law of rational beings, to whom freedom of the causality of their will is ascribed. This is because the two concepts are so inextricably bound together that practical freedom could be defined through the will's independence of everything except the [94] moral law. But the possibility of freedom of an efficient cause cannot be comprehended, especially in the world of sense; we are indeed fortunate if we can be sufficiently assured that no proof of its impossibility can be given and that the moral law postulates freedom and compels and authorizes us to assume it.

But there are many who believe they can explain this freedom with empirical principles, just as they can explain other natural abilities. They regard it as a psychological property, the explanation of which turns solely upon a more exact investigation of the nature of the soul and of the drives of the will and not as the transcendental predicate of the causality of a being which belongs to the world of sense; but it is this latter which is what really counts. Thus they deprive us of the great revelation which we experience through pure practical reason by means of the moral law—the revelation of an intelligible world through realization of the otherwise transcendent concept of freedom; they deprive us of moral law itself, which assumes absolutely no empirical motive. Therefore, it will be necessary to add something here as a protection against this delusion and to expose empiricism in its naked superficiality.

The concept of causality as natural necessity, unlike the concept of causality as freedom, concerns only the existence of things as far as it is determinable in time, and consequently as appearances in contrast to their causality as things in themselves. If one takes the attributes of the existence of things in time for attributes of things in themselves, which is the usual way of thinking, the necessity in the causal relation can in no way be united with freedom. They are contradictory to each other, for the former implies that every event, and consequently every action which occurs at a certain point of time, is necessary under the condition of what preceded it. Since the past is no longer in my power, every action which I perform is necessary because of determining grounds which are not in my power. That means that at the time I act I am never free. Indeed, if I assumed my entire existence were independent of any external cause (e.g., God), so that the determining grounds [95] of my causality and even of my whole existence were not outside me, this would not in the least convert that natural necessity into freedom. For at every point of time I still stand under the necessity of being determined to act by what is not in my power, and the *a parte priori* infinite series of events which I can continue only by an already predetermined order would never commence of itself. It would be a continuous natural chain, and thus my causality would never be freedom.

Therefore, if one attributes freedom to a being whose existence is determined in time, its existence, including its actions, cannot be exempted from the law of natural necessity of all events in its existence, including also its actions. Making such an exception would be equivalent to delivering this being to blind chance. Since this law inevitably concerns all causality of things so far as their existence is determinable in time, freedom would have to be rejected as a void and impossible concept if this were the way in which we thought of the existence of these things as they are in themselves. Consequently, if we wish still to save it, no other course remains than to ascribe the existence of a thing so far as it is determinable in time, and accordingly its causality under the law of natural necessity, merely to appearance, and to attribute freedom to the same being as a thing in itself. This is absolutely unavoidable if one wishes to maintain both these mutually incompatible concepts; but in applying them, when one wishes to explain them as united in one and the same action and thus explain this union itself, great difficulties turn up, which seem to make such a unification impossible.

Suppose I say of a man who has committed a theft that this act, by the natural law of causality, is a necessary result of the determining ground existing in the preceding time and that it was therefore impossible that it could have not been done. How, then, can judgment according to the moral law make any change in it? And how can it be supposed that it still could have been left undone because the law says that it ought to have been left undone? That is, how can he be called free at this point of time with reference to this action, when in this moment and in this action he stands under inexorable natural necessity? It is a wretched subterfuge to seek an escape in [96] the supposition that the *kind* of determining grounds of his causality according to natural law agrees with a comparative concept of freedom. According to this concept, what is sometimes called "free effect" is that of which the determining natural cause is internal to the acting thing. For example, that which a projectile performs when it is in free motion is called by the name "freedom" because it is not pushed by anything external while it is in flight. Or, another example: we call the motion of a clock "free movement" because it moves the hands itself, which need not be pushed by an external force. So one might call the actions of man "free" because they are actions caused by ideas we have produced by our own powers, whereby desires are evoked on occasion of circumstances and thus because they are actions brought about at our own pleasure; in this sense they are called free even though they are necessary because their determining grounds have preceded them in time. With this manner of argument many allow themselves to be put off and believe that with a little quibbling they have found the solution to the difficult problem which millennia have sought in vain and which could hardly be expected to be found so completely on the surface.

In the question of freedom which lies at the foundation of all moral laws and accountability to them, it is really not at all a question of whether the causality determined by a natural law is necessary through determining grounds lying within or without the subject, or whether, if they lie within him, they are in instinct or in motives thought by reason. If these determining representations themselves have the ground of their existence in time and, more particularly, in the antecedent state and these again in a preceding state, and so on (as these men themselves admit); and if they are without exception internal; and if they do not have mechanical causality but a psychological causality through representations instead of through bodily movements: they are nonetheless determining grounds of the causality of a being so far as his existence is determinable in time. As such, this being is under necessitating conditions of past time which are no longer in his power when he acts. Thus these conceptions do indeed imply psychological freedom (if one wishes to use this word for a merely internal concatenation of representations in the mind), but nonetheless they also imply natural necessity, leaving no room for transcendental freedom which must be thought of as independence from [97] everything empirical and hence from nature generally, whether regarded as an object of inner sense merely in time or also as an object of outer sense in both space and time. Without transcendental freedom in its proper meaning, which is alone a priori practical, no moral law and no accountability to it are possible. For this reason, all necessity of events in time according to natural law can be called the "mechanism of nature," even though it is not supposed that things which are subject to it must really be material machines. Here reference is made only to the necessity of the connection of events in a temporal series as they develop according to natural law, whether the subject in which this development occurs be called *automaton materiale* when the machinery is impelled by matter, or, with Leibniz, *automaton spirituale* when it is impelled by representations. And if the freedom of our will were nothing else than the latter, i.e., psychological and comparative and not at the same time also transcendental or absolute, it would in essence be no better than the freedom of a turnspit, which when once wound up also carries out its motions of itself.

Now in order to remove the apparent contradiction between

the mechanism of nature and freedom in the case under discussion, we must remember what was said in the *Critique of
Pure Reason* or what it implies, viz., that natural necessity,
which cannot coexist with the freedom of the subject, attaches
merely to the determinations of a thing which stands under the
conditions of time, and consequently applies only to the determination of the acting subject as appearance. As a consequence, [natural necessity pertains to the subject] only so far as
the determining grounds of any action of the subject lie in what
belongs to the past and is no longer in his power; in this must
be counted also his already performed acts and his character as
a phenomenon as this is determinable for him in his own eyes
by those acts. But the same subject, which, on the other hand, is
conscious also of his own existence as a thing in itself, also
views his existence *so far as it does not stand under temporal
conditions*, and himself as determinable only by laws which he
gives to himself through reason. In this his existence nothing is
antecedent to the determination of his will; every action and, in
general, every changing determination of his existence conformable to inner sense, even the entire history of his [98]
existence as a sensuous being, is seen in the consciousness of
his intelligible existence as nothing but a consequence, not as a
determining ground, of his causality as a noumenon. From this
point of view, a rational being can rightly say of any unlawful
action that he has done that he could have left it undone, even if
as an appearance it was sufficiently determined in the past and
thus far was inescapably necessary. For this action and everything in the past which determined it belong to a single phenomenon of his character, which he himself creates, and according to which he imputes to himself, as a cause
independent of all sensuousness, the causality of those
appearances.

The judicial sentences of that marvelous faculty in us called
conscience are in complete agreement with this. A man may
dissemble as much as he will in order to paint his remembered
unlawful behavior as an unintentional error, as mere oversight,
which can never be entirely avoided, and consequently as

something to which he was carried along by the stream of natural necessity, and in this way try to make himself out as innocent. But he finds that the advocate who speaks in his behalf cannot silence the accuser in him when he is conscious that at the time when he committed the wrong he was in his senses, i.e., he was in possession of his freedom. Nevertheless, he explains his misdeed by some bad habits which he has grown into by gradual neglect of attention to such a degree that he can regard the act as a natural consequence of them, but this cannot protect him from the blame and the reproach he casts upon himself. On this is based the repentance for an action long past, every time he remembers it. It is a painful feeling caused by the moral disposition, empty in a practical sense since it cannot undo that which has been done. Priestley,[4] as a true and consistent fatalist, even declares it to be absurd, and he deserves more applause for his candor than those who, asserting the mechanism of the will in acts but affirming its freedom in words, wish to have it thought that they include it in their syncretistic [99] system, though they cannot render the possibility of such an imputation comprehensible. But as pain, repentance is entirely legitimate, because reason, when it is a question of the law of our intelligible existence (the moral law), acknowledges no temporal distinctions and only asks whether the event belongs to me as my act, and then morally connects with it the same feeling, whether the event occurs now or is long since past. For the life of the senses is but a single phenomenon in the eyes of an intelligible consciousness of its existence (the consciousness of freedom), and this phenomenon, so far as it contains merely appearances of the disposition which is of concern to the moral law (i.e., appearances of character), must be judged not according to natural necessity which pertains to it as appearance but according to the absolute spontaneity of freedom.

It may be admitted that if it were possible for us to have so deep an insight into a man's character as shown both in inner

[4]Joseph Priestley, *The Doctrine of Philosophical Necessity Illustrated* (1777).

and in outer actions, that every, even the least, drive to these actions and all external occasions which affect them were so known to us that his future conduct could be predicted with as great a certainty as the occurrence of a solar or lunar eclipse, we could nevertheless still assert that the man is free. For if we were capable of another view (which, however, is certainly not given us, but in place of which we have only the concept of reason), i.e., if we were capable of an intellectual intuition of the same subject, we would then discover that the entire chain of appearances, with reference to that which concerns only the moral law, depends upon the spontaneity of the subject as a thing in itself, for the determination of which no physical explanation can be given. Lacking this intuition, the moral law assures us of this difference between the relation of our actions as appearances to the sense-being of our subject and the relation by which this sensuous being is itself connected to the intelligible substrate in us.

From this point of view, which is natural although inexplicable to our reason, judgments may be justified which, though made in all conscientiousness, seem at first glance to conflict with equity. There are cases in which men, even with an education which was profitable to others, have shown while still children such depravity, which continues to grow during their adult years, that they are held to be born villains and incapable of any improvement of character; yet they are judged by [100] their acts, they are reproached as guilty of their crimes; and, indeed, they themselves (the children) find these reproaches as well grounded as if they, regardless of the hopeless quality ascribed to their minds, were just as responsible as any other men. This could not happen if we did not suppose that whatever arises from man's choice (as every intentional act undoubtedly does) has a free causality as its ground, which from early youth expresses its character in its appearances (its actions). These actions, by the uniformity of conduct, exhibit a natural connection. But the latter does not render the vicious quality of the will necessary, for this quality is rather the consequence of freely assumed evil and unchangeable principles. This fact makes it only the more objectionable and culpable.

But there is still another difficulty in the way of freedom so far as it is to be united with the mechanism of nature in a being belonging to the world of sense. Even after all the foregoing has been agreed to, it is a difficulty which threatens freedom with its complete downfall. But in this danger, one circumstance gives hope for a successful outcome to the asseveration of freedom, namely, that the same difficulty presses even stronger (and in fact, as we shall soon see, only) on the system in which the existence that is determinable in time and space is held to be existence of finite things in themselves. Therefore, this difficulty does not compel us to give up our principal presupposition of the ideality of time as a mere form of sensible intuition and thus as only a mode of representation proper to the subject as belonging to the world of sense. It only demands, on the contrary, that this presupposition be united with the Idea of freedom.

[This difficulty is as follows.] If it be conceded that the intelligible subject can be free with reference to a given action, even though as a subject belonging to the world of sense it is mechanically determined to this action, it nevertheless appears that as soon as it is assumed that God as the Universal Primordial Being is the cause also of the existence of substance (and this assumption can never be given up without surrendering the concept of God as the Being of all Beings and thus His all-sufficiency, on which everything in theology is based), one must also grant that the actions of a man have their deter- [101] mining ground in something completely beyond his own power, i.e., in the causality of a Highest Being which is different from him and upon which his existence and the entire determination of his causality absolutely depend. Actually, if the actions of man, as they pertain to his determinations in time, were not merely properties of his being as appearance but also of his being as a thing regarded as he is in himself, freedom could not be saved. Man would be a marionette or an automaton like Vaucanson's,[5] fabricated and wound up by the Supreme Artist; self-consciousness would indeed make him a thinking automaton, but the consciousness of his spontaneity, if this is held to be freedom, would be a mere illusion. It would deserve to be called so only comparatively, as the proximate determining causes of its movement and a long series of their determining causes would be internal, while the ultimate and highest would lie wholly in a foreign hand. Therefore, I cannot conceive how those who persist in seeing space and time as attributes belonging to the existence of things in themselves can avoid fatalism of actions. Or, when they (like the otherwise so acute Mendelssohn)[6] concede both as necessarily belonging to the existence of finite and derived beings, but not that of the infinite First Being, I do not see how they justify themselves or where they get the right to make such a distinction. I do not see even how they can evade the contradiction into which they fall when they regard existence in time as an attribute necessarily pertaining to finite things in themselves. This contradiction is as follows. God is the cause of this existence, and yet He cannot be the cause of time (or space) itself (because, as the necessary condition a priori for the existence of things, it must be presupposed [by this hypothesis]); consequently, God's causation of the existence of these things would have to be conditioned—in fact, temporally conditioned. Thereby everything which contradicts the concept of His infinity and independence would be unavoidably brought in.

It is very easy for us, on the other hand, to differentiate between the attribute of divine existence as independent of all temporal conditions and that of a being in the world of sense, as this distinction is precisely that between the existence of a being in itself and that of a thing in appearance. Therefore, if the ideality of time and space is not assumed, only [102]

---

[5]A. von Vaucanson had exhibited automatic figures in Paris in 1738.

[6]Moses Mendelssohn (1729–1786), a German philosopher much admired by Kant, in his *Morgenstunden* (1786).

Spinozism remains, which holds space and time to be essential attributes of the First Being itself and the things dependent upon it (ourselves included), to be not substances but merely accidents inhering in substance. For if these things exist only as its effects in time, which would then be the condition of their existence itself, the actions of these beings would have to be merely the actions of one substance which it performs anywhere and at any time. Spinozism, therefore, in spite of the absurdity of its basic idea, argues far more cogently than the creation theory can when the latter sees beings which have been presumed to be substances existing in themselves in time as effects of a supreme cause, yet not as belonging to it and to its action but as substances in themselves.

The difficulty mentioned above is resolved briefly and clearly as follows. If existence in time is merely a sensible mode of presentation belonging to thinking beings in the world, and consequently does not concern them as things in themselves, the creation of these beings is a creation of things in themselves, because the concept of creation does not belong to the sensible mode of conceiving of existence or causality but can be referred only to noumena. Consequently, if I say of beings in the world of sense that they are created, I regard them only as noumena. Just as it would therefore be contradictory to say God is the creator of appearances, it is also a contradiction to say that He, as the creator, is the cause of actions in the world of sense, as these are appearances; yet at the same time He is the cause of the existence of the acting beings (as noumena). Now, assuming existence in time to hold only of appearances and not of things in themselves, if it is possible to affirm freedom without detriment to the natural mechanism of actions as appearances, then the circumstance that the acting beings are creatures cannot make the least difference to the argument, because creation concerns their intelligible but not their sensible existence, and therefore creation cannot be regarded as the determining ground of appearances. It would turn out very differently if the beings in the world existed as things in themselves in time, since the creator of substance would then be also the author of the entire mechanism of this substance.

Such is the importance of the separation of time (as [103] well as space) from the existence of things in themselves, as this was effected in the *Critique of Pure* (speculative) *Reason*.

The solution which is given here to the difficulty will be said to have so much difficulty in it, however, that it is hardly susceptible of a lucid presentation. But is any other solution, which anyone has attempted or may attempt, any easier or more comprehensible? Rather might we say that the dogmatic teachers of metaphysics have shown more shrewdness than frankness in removing this difficult point as far as possible from view in the hope that, if they did not speak of it, no one would be likely to think of it. But, if a science is to be advanced, all difficulties must be exposed, and those which lie hidden in its way must even be sought out, for each of them calls forth a remedy without which means cannot be found to advance the science, whether in scope or in accuracy. In this way even obstacles will be means for furthering the thoroughness of the science. But, if, on the contrary, difficulties are intentionally hidden or merely removed with palliatives, sooner or later they break out in incurable evils, which bring the science to ruin in complete skepticism.

Since among all the Ideas of pure speculative reason it is, properly speaking, only the concept of freedom which brings such a great extension in the field of the supersensible, though it is only practical knowledge which is enlarged, I ask myself: Why does it alone have such great fruitfulness, the others only indicating the empty place for merely possible beings of the understanding without being able in any way to define the concept of them? I soon see that, since I can think nothing without a category, I must first seek out the category in reason's Idea of freedom. This is the category of causality. I also see that, although no corresponding intuition can be made the basis of *reason's* concept of freedom, inasmuch as it is a transcendent concept, a sensible intuition must previously be given to the *understanding's* concept of causality (for the synthesis of which *reason's* concept of freedom requires the unconditioned), and only by sensible intuition is it assured objective reality.

Now all categories are divided into two classes: the [104] mathematical, which deal with the unity of synthesis in the representation of objects, and the dynamical, which concern the synthetic unity in the representation of the existence of objects. The former (the categories of quantity and quality) always contain a synthesis of the homogeneous, in which the unconditioned for the sensibly conditioned cannot be found, since the unconditioned would itself be in space and time and thus would itself still be conditioned. Therefore, in the Dialectic of pure theoretical reason, the contrasted ways of finding the unconditioned and the totality of conditions for it were both false. The categories of the second class (those of causality and of the necessity of a thing) did in no way require this homogeneity of the conditioned and the condition in synthesis, because here it was not a question of how intuition is synthesized from a manifold within it but only of how existence of the conditioned object corresponding to the intuition is added to the existence of the condition (added in the understanding, as connected with it). In these categories it was permitted to add to the completely conditioned in the world of sense (to the causality and the contingent existence of things) the unconditioned in the intelligible world and to make the synthesis transcendent; this was permissible, even though the unconditioned was not further defined. Therefore, in the Dialectic of pure speculative reason it was found that the two apparently incompatible modes of finding the unconditioned for the conditioned (e.g., in the synthesis of causality, to find a causality which has no sensible condition for the conditioned in the series of causes and effects in the world of sense) do not in fact contradict each other; and that the same act, which as belonging to the world of sense is always sensibly conditioned, i.e., mechanically necessary, can at the same time, as belonging to the causality of the acting being in so far as it belongs to the intelligible world, have a sensibly unconditioned causality as its foundation. That is, it can be thought of as free.

Then it was only a question of whether this "can be" could be changed to an "is"; it was a question of whether in an actual case and, as it were, by a fact, one could prove that certain actions presupposed such an intellectual, sensibly unconditioned, causality, regardless of whether they are actual or only commanded, i.e., objectively and practically necessary. In actions actually given in experience as events in the world of sense we could not hope to meet with this connection, [105] since causality through freedom must always be sought outside the world of sense in the intelligible, and things which are not sensible are not given to our perception and observation. Thus nothing remained but that perhaps an incontrovertible, objective principle of causality could be found which excluded every sensible condition from its determination, i.e., a principle in which reason does not call upon anything else as the determining ground of causality but rather by that principle itself contains it, thus being, as pure reason, practical of itself. This principle, however, needs no search and no invention, having long been in the reason of all men and embodied in their being. It is the principle of morality. Therefore, that unconditioned causality and its faculty, freedom, and therewith a being (myself) which belongs to the world of sense and at the same time to the intelligible world, are no longer thought merely indeterminately and problematically (which even speculative reason could admit as possible), but with respect to the law of its causality are determinately and assertorically known; thus is the reality of the intelligible world definitely established from a practical point of view, and this determinateness, which would be transcendent (extravagant) for theoretical purposes, is for practical purposes immanent.

We could not, however, take this step with the second dynamical Idea, i.e., that of a necessary being. Without the mediation of the first dynamical Idea we could not rise to it from the world of sense. For if we wish to try it, we should have to make the venture of leaving everything which is given to us and to plunge into that of which nothing is given to us by which we could mediate the connection of such an intelligible being with the world of sense (because the necessary being would be known as given *outside* us). Nevertheless, with respect to our own subject so far as we know ourselves, on the one hand, as intelligible beings determined because of their freedom by the moral law, and, on the other, as acting according to this determination in the world of sense, it is obvious that all this is quite possible. Only the concept of freedom enables us to find the unconditioned for the conditioned and the intelligible for the sensible without going outside ourselves. For it is our [106] reason itself which through the supreme and unconditioned practical law recognizes itself, and the being which knows this law (our own person) as belonging to the pure world of the understanding and indeed defines the way in which it can be active as such a being. Thus it can be seen why in the entire faculty of reason only the practical can lift us above the world of sense and furnish cognitions of a supersensible order and connection, though these cognitions can be extended only as far as is needed for pure practical purposes.

Here I wish to call attention, if I may, to one thing, namely, that every step which one takes with pure reason, even in the practical field where one does not take subtle speculation into account, so neatly and naturally dovetails with all parts of the *Critique of Pure* (theoretical) *Reason* that it is as if each step had been carefully thought out merely to establish this confirmation. This agreement was by no means sought after. It is rather (as one can convince himself if he only follows moral considerations back to their principles) a self-evident agreement between the most important propositions of practical reason with the often seemingly too subtle and unnecessary remarks of the *Critique of Pure* (speculative) *Reason*—an accord that occasions surprise and astonishment, strengthening the maxim, already known and recommended by others, that in every scientific investigation we should unswervingly pursue our course with all possible accuracy and candor without attending to any extraneous difficulties it might involve, carrying

out as far as we can our investigation by itself honestly and completely. Frequent observation has convinced me that once one
has seen through such business, that which, when half-fin-
ished, appeared very dubious in view of extraneous theories, is
at last found to be in an unexpected way completely harmonious with that which had been discovered separately without
the least regard for them, provided this dubiousness is left out
of sight for a while and only the business at hand is attended to
until it is finished. Writers would save themselves many errors
and much labor lost (because spent on delusions) if they could
only resolve to go to work with a little more ingenuousness.

BOOK II
DIALECTIC OF PURE PRACTICAL REASON

CHAPTER I

OF A DIALECTIC OF PURE PRACTICAL REASON IN GENERAL

In both its speculative and its practical employment, [107] pure reason always has its dialectic, for it demands the absolute totality of conditions for a given conditioned thing, and this can be reached only in things in themselves. Since, however, all concepts of things must be referred to intuitions which, for us human beings, can never be other than sensible, and which thus let objects be known not as things in themselves but only as appearances, appearances being a series of the conditioned and their conditions in which the unconditioned can never be found, it follows that an unavoidable illusions arises from the application of the rational Idea of the totality of conditions (and thus of the unconditioned) to appearances as if they were things in themselves (for this is the way in which they are considered in default of a warning critique). But the illusion would never be noticed as deceptive if it were not betrayed by a conflict of reason with itself in applying to appearances its principle of presupposing the unconditioned for every conditioned thing. Reason is thus forced to investigate this illusion, to find out how it arises and how it can be removed. This can be done only through a complete critical examination of the entire pure faculty of reason; the antinomy of pure reason, which becomes obvious in its dialectic, is, in fact, the most fortunate perplexity in which human reason could ever have become involved, since it finally compels us to seek the key to escape from this labyrinth. This key, when once found, discovers that which we did not seek and yet need, namely, a view into a higher immutable order of things in which we already are and may continue to exist in accordance with the supreme decree of reason; to this end, after this discovery, we may be directed by defi- [108] nite precepts.

How to solve that natural dialectic and to avoid the error arising from an otherwise natural illusion in the speculative use of pure reason can be found in detail in the *Critique* of that faculty. But reason in its practical use is not a bit better off. As pure practical reason it likewise seeks the unconditioned for the practically conditioned (which rests on inclinations and natural need); and this unconditioned is not only sought as the determining ground of the will but, even when this is given (in the moral law), it is also sought as the unconditioned totality of the object of pure practical reason, under the name of the *highest good.*

To define this idea practically, i.e., sufficiently for the maxims of our rational conduct, is [the task of] the doctrine of wisdom, which, as a science, is philosophy in the sense in which the ancients understood this word, for whom it meant instruction in the concept wherein the highest good was to be placed and in the conduct by which it was to be obtained. It would be well if we left this word with its old meaning, as a doctrine of the highest good so far as reason strives to being it to [the level of] science. For, on the one hand, the qualifying condition would be suitable to the Greek expression (which means love of *wisdom*), and yet entirely adequate to comprehend under the name of philosophy the love of *science,* and thus of all speculative rational knowledge, so far as it is serviceable to reason [in defining] that concept and the practical motive; [it could do all this] without letting us lose sight of the chief goal for the sake of which alone it is called a doctrine of wisdom. On the other hand, it would also do no harm to deter the self-conceit of whoever presumed to the title of philosopher, if one merely held before him the definition as the standard for his self-estimation, as this would lower his pretensions very much. For to be a teacher of wisdom would mean something more than to be a student, who has not yet progressed far enough to conduct himself, and even less anyone else, to so high an end; it would mean to be *a master of the knowledge of wisdom*, which says more than a modest man would himself presume to claim. Philosophy as well as wisdom itself would always remain an ideal, which objectively is repre- [109] sented completely only in reason and which subjectively is only the goal for the person's unceasing endeavors. No one would be justified in professing to be in possession of it, under the assumed name of philosopher, unless he could show its infallible effect (in self-mastery and the unquestioned interest which he pre-eminently takes in the general good) on his own person as an example. This the ancients required as a condition for deserving that honorable title.

We have to make only one more preliminary remark with respect to the dialectic of pure practical reason in its definition of the concept of the highest good; and, if the solution of this dialectic is attained, we may expect a result just as useful as that accruing from the dialectic of theoretical reason, since the self-contradictions of pure practical reason, if properly exposed and not concealed, impel us to an exhaustive critical examination of its capacities.

The moral law is the sole motive of the pure will. Since it is merely formal, requiring only that the form of the maxim be that of universal law, as a determining ground it abstracts from all material and thus from every object of volition. Consequently, though the highest good may be the entire *object* of pure practical reason, i.e., of a pure will, it is still not to be taken as the *motive* of the pure will; the moral law alone must be seen as the ground for making the highest good and its realization or promotion the object of the pure will. This reminder is of importance in a case as delicate as that of the definition of moral principles, where even the slightest mistake perverts the character. For one sees from the Analytic that when we assume any object, under the name of good, as the motive of the will prior to the moral law, and then derive the supreme practical principle from it, this always produces heteronomy and rules out the moral principle.

But it is self-evident not merely that, if the moral law is included as the supreme condition in the concept of the highest good, the highest good is then the object, but also that the concept of it and the representation of its existence as pos- [110] sible through our practical reason are at the same time the motive of the pure will. This is because the moral law, included and thought in this concept, and no other object, determines the will as required by the principle of autonomy. This order of concepts of the determination of the will should not be lost sight of, for otherwise we misunderstand ourselves and believe we are contradicting ourselves when everything really stands in the most perfect harmony.

CHAPTER II

ON THE DIALECTIC OF PURE REASON IN DEFINING THE CONCEPT OF THE HIGHEST GOOD

The concept of "highest" contains an ambiguity which, if not attended to, can occasion unnecessary disputes. The "highest" can mean the "supreme" (*supremum*) or the "perfect" (*consummatum*). The former is the unconditional condition, i.e., the condition which is subordinate to no other (*originarium*); the latter is that whole which is no part of a yet larger whole of the same kind (*perfectissimum*). That virtue (as the worthiness to be happy) is the supreme condition of whatever appears to us to be desirable and thus of all our pursuit of happiness and, consequently, that it is the supreme good have been proved in the Analytic. But these truths do not imply that virtue is the entire and perfect good as the object of the faculty of desire of rational finite beings. For this, happiness is also required, and indeed not merely in the partial eyes of a person who makes himself his end but even in the judgment of an impartial reason, which impartially regards persons in the world as ends in themselves. For to be in need of happiness and also worthy of it and yet not to partake of it could not be in accordance with the perfect volition of an omnipotent rational being, if we assume such only for the sake of the argument. Inasmuch as virtue and happiness together constitute the possession of the highest good for one person, and happiness in exact proportion to morality (as the worth of a person and his worthiness to be happy) constitutes that of a possible world, the highest good means the whole, the perfect good, wherein virtue is always the [111] supreme good, being the condition having no condition superior to it, while happiness, though something always pleasant to him who possesses it, is not of itself absolutely good in every respect but always presupposes conduct in accordance with the moral law as its condition.

Two terms necessarily combined in one concept must be related as ground and consequent, and this unity must be regarded either as analytic (logical connection) according to the law of identity or as synthetic (real connection) according to the law of causality. The connection of virtue with happiness can, therefore, be understood in one of two ways. Either the endeavor to be virtuous and the rational pursuit of happiness are not two different actions but absolutely identical; in this case no maxim is needed as a ground of the former other than that needed for the latter. Or that connection is predicated upon virtue's producing happiness as something different from the consciousness of virtue, as a cause produces an effect.

Of the ancient Greek schools, there were only two opposing each other on this issue. But so far as the definition of the concept of the highest good is concerned, they followed one and the same method, since neither held virtue and happiness to be two different elements of the highest good, but both sought the unity of principle under the rule of identity. But again they differed in that each selected a different principle as the fundamental one. The Epicurean said: To be conscious of one's maxims as leading to happiness is virtue. The Stoic said: To be conscious of one's virtue is happiness. To the former, prudence amounted to morality; to the latter, who chose a higher term for virtue, morality alone was true wisdom.

We cannot but regret that these men (whom we must nevertheless admire since they so early attempted all the conceivable ways of extending philosophy's conquest) unfortunately applied their acuteness to digging up an identity between such extremely heterogeneous concepts as those of happiness and virtue. But it fit the dialectical spirit of their times (and still sometimes leads subtle minds astray) to overcome essential differences in principle, which can never be united, by seeking to translate them into a conflict of words and thus to devise an apparent unity of the concepts with other terms. This [112] commonly occurs in cases where the unification of heterogeneous principles lies either so high or so deep, or would require so thorough a revolution of doctrines otherwise accepted in a philosophical system, that men fear to go deeply into the real difference and prefer to treat it as a mere diversity in formulas.

While both schools tried to ferret out the sameness of the practical principles of virtue and happiness, they were not for that reason agreed as to the way in which to force out this identity; rather they became widely separated from each other, as the one sought its principle on the sensuous and the other on the logical side, one putting it in the consciousness of sensuous need and the other in the independence of practical reason from all sensuous motives. The concept of virtue, according to the Epicurean, lay already in the maxim of furthering one's own happiness; the feeling of happiness, for the Stoic, was, on the contrary, already contained in the consciousness of his virtue. Whatever is contained in another concept, however, is the same as one of its parts but not the same as the whole, and two wholes can, moreover, be specifically different from each other though they consist of the same content if their parts are combined in different ways. The Stoic asserted virtue to be the entire highest good, and happiness was only the consciousness of this possession as belonging to the state of the subject. The

Epicurean stated that happiness was the entire highest good and that virtue was only the form of the maxim by which it could be procured through the rational use of means to it.

But it is clear from the Analytic that the maxims of virtue and those of one's own happiness are wholly heterogeneous and far removed from being at one in respect to their supreme practical principle; and even though they belong to a highest good, which they jointly make possible, they strongly limit and check each other in the same subject. Thus the question, "How is the highest good practically possible?" remains an unsolved problem in spite of all previous attempts at conciliation. That which makes it so difficult a problem is shown in the Analytic: happiness and morality are two specifically different elements of the highest good and therefore their combination cannot be known analytically (as if a person who sought his happi- [113] ness found himself virtuous merely through solving his problem, or one who followed virtue found himself *ipso facto* happy in the consciousness of this conduct). The highest good is a *synthesis* of concepts. Since, however, this combination is known as a priori and thus as practically necessary, and not derivable from experience, and since the possibility of the highest good therefore rests on no empirical principles, the deduction of this concept must be transcendental. It is a priori (morally) necessary *to bring forth the highest good through the freedom of the will*; the condition of its possibility, therefore, must rest solely on a priori grounds of knowledge.

I. THE ANTINOMY OF PRACTICAL REASON

In the highest good which is practical for us, i.e., one which is to be made real by our will, virtue and happiness are thought of as necessarily combined, so that the one cannot be assumed by a practical reason without the other belonging to it. Now this combination is, like every other, either analytic or synthetic. Since it cannot be analytic, as has been shown, it must be thought synthetically and, more particularly, as the connection of cause and effect, for it concerns a practical good, i.e., one that is possible through action. Therefore, the desire for happiness must be the motive to maxims of virtue, or the maxim of virtue must be the efficient cause of happiness. The first is absolutely impossible, because (as has been proved in the Analytic) maxims which put the determining ground of the will in the desire for one's happiness are not moral at all and can serve as ground for no virtue. The second is, however, also impossible, since every practical connection of causes and effects in the world, as a result of the determination of the will, is dependent not on the moral dispositions of the will but on knowledge of natural laws and the physical capacity of using them to its purposes; consequently, no necessary connection, sufficient to the highest good, between happiness and virtue in the world can be expected from the most meticulous observance of the moral law. Since, now, the furthering of the highest [114] good, which contains this connection in its concept, is an a priori necessary object of our will and is inseparably related to the moral law, the impossibility of the highest good must prove the falsity of the moral law also. If, therefore, the highest good is impossible according to practical rules, then the moral law which commands that it be furthered must be fantastic, directed to empty imaginary ends, and consequently inherently false.

II. CRITICAL RESOLUTION OF THE ANTINOMY OF PRACTICAL REASON

In the antinomy of pure speculative reason there is a similar conflict between natural necessity and freedom in the causation of events in the world. It was resolved by showing that there is no true conflict if the events and even the world in which they occur are regarded as only appearances (as they should be). This is because one and the same acting being as appearance (even to his own inner sense) has a causality in the sensible world always in accord with the mechanism of nature; while with respect to the same event, as far as the acting person regards himself as noumenon (as pure intelligence, existing without temporal determination), he can contain a determining ground of that causality which holds under natural laws, and this determining ground of natural causality itself is free from every natural law.

It is just the same with the present antinomy of pure practical reason. The first of the two propositions, viz., that striving for happiness produces a ground for a virtuous disposition, is absolutely false; the second, viz., that a virtuous disposition necessarily produces happiness, is not, however, *absolutely* false but false only in so far as this disposition is regarded as the form of causality in the world of sense. Consequently, it is false only if I assume existence in this world to be the only mode of existence of a rational being, and therefore it is only *conditionally* false. But not only since I am justified in thinking of my existence as that of a noumenon in an intelligible world but also since I have in the moral law a pure intellectual deter- [115] mining ground of my causality (in the sensuous world), it is not impossible that the morality of disposition should have a necessary relation as cause to happiness as an effect in the sensuous world; but this relation is indirect, mediated by an intelligible Author of nature. This combination, however, can occur only contingently in a system of nature which is merely the object of the senses and as such not sufficient to the highest good.

Thus, in spite of this apparent conflict of a practical reason with itself, the highest good is the necessary highest end of a morally determined will and a true object thereof; for it is practically possible, and the maxims of this will, which refer to it by their material, have objective reality. At first this objective reality was called in question by the antinomy in the combination of morality with happiness according to a general law; but this difficulty arose only from a misconception, because the relationship between appearances was held to be a relationship of the things in themselves to these appearances.

When we see ourselves obliged to seek at such distance — namely, in the context of an intelligible world — the possibility of the highest good which reason presents to all rational beings as the goal of all their moral wishes, it must appear strange that philosophers of both ancient and modern times have been able to find happiness in very just proportion to virtue in *this* life (in the world of sense) or at least have been able to convince themselves of it. For Epicurus as well as the Stoics extolled happiness springing from the consciousness of virtuous living above everything else, and the former was not so base in his practical precepts as one might conclude from the principles of his theory, which he used for explanation and not for action, or from the principles as interpreted by many who were misled by his use of the term "pleasure" for "contentment." He, on the contrary, reckoned the most disinterested practice of the good among the ways of experiencing the most intimate joy; and moderation and control of the inclinations, as these might have been required by the strictest moral philosopher, belonged in his scheme for enjoyment, whereby he understood constant cheerfulness. He diverged from the Stoics chiefly by placing the *motive* in this enjoyment, which the Stoics correctly refused to do. For the virtuous Epicurus, like even now [116] many morally well-meaning persons who do not give deep enough consideration to their principles, fell into the error of presupposing the virtuous disposition to be already in the persons to whom he wished to provide drives to virtue. It is true that the upright man cannot be happy if he is not already conscious of his righteousness, since with such a character the moral self-condemnation to which his own way of thinking would force him in case of any transgression would rob him of all enjoyment of the pleasantness which his condition might otherwise entail. But the only question is, "How is such a character and turn of mind in estimating the worth of his existence even possible?" For prior to this no feeling for any moral worth can be found in a subject. However favorable fortune may be to a man in the physical circumstances of his life, if he is virtuous he will certainly not enjoy life without being conscious of his righteousness in each action; but can one make him virtuous before he has so high an estimation of the moral worth of his existence merely by commending to him the contentment of spirit which will arise from the consciousness of righteousness for which he as yet has no sense?

But, on the other hand, there is always here an occasion for a subreption (*vitium subreptionis*) and, as it were, for an optical illusion in the self-consciousness of what one does in contradistinction to what one feels, which even the most experienced person cannot entirely avoid. The moral disposition is necessarily connected with a consciousness of the determination of the will directly by a law. Now the consciousness of a determination of the faculty of desire is always a ground for satisfaction in the resulting action; but this pleasure, this satisfaction with one's self, is not the motive of the action; on the contrary, the determination of the will directly by reason alone is the ground of the feeling of pleasure, and this remains a pure practical determination of the faculty of desire, not a sensuous one. Since this determination produces the same inward effect, i.e., an impulse to activity, as does a feeling of agreeableness which is expected from the desired action, we see that what we ourselves do may easily be looked upon as something which we merely passively feel, the moral motive being held to be a [117] sensuous impulse, as it always occurs in so-called illusions of the senses (and here we have such an illusion of the inner sense). It is a very sublime thing in human nature to be determined to actions directly by a pure law of reason, and even the illusion wherein the subjective element of this intellectual determinability of the will is held to be sensuous and an effect of a particular sensuous feeling ("intellectual feeling" being self-contradictory) partakes of this sublimity. It is of great importance to point out this quality of our personality and to cultivate so far as possible the effect of reason on this feeling. But we must, nevertheless, be on guard against degrading and deforming the real and authentic drive, the law itself, by awarding spurious praise to the moral motive as the drive as though it were based on feelings of particular joys, thus setting it, as it were, against a false foil; for these joys are only its consequences. Respect, in contrast to the enjoyment or gratification of happiness, is something for which there can be no feeling basic and prior to reason, for such a feeling would always be sensuous and pathological. Respect as the consciousness of the direct constraint of the will through law is hardly analogous to the feeling of pleasure, although in relation to the faculty of desire it produces exactly the same effect, but from different sources. But only through this mode of conception can one achieve what is sought, namely, that actions be done not merely according to duty (as a consequence of pleasant feelings) but from duty, which must be the true goal of all moral cultivation.

Do we not have a word to denote a satisfaction with existence, an analogue of happiness which necessarily accompanies the consciousness of virtue, and which does not indicate a [sensuous] gratification, as "happiness" does? We do, and this word is "self-contentment," which in its real meaning refers only to negative satisfaction with existence in which one is conscious of needing nothing. Freedom and the consciousness of freedom, as a capacity for following the moral law with an unyielding disposition, are independent from inclinations, at least as motives determining (though not as affecting) our desiring; and, so far as I am conscious of freedom in obeying my moral maxims, it is the exclusive source of an unchanging contentment necessarily connected with it and resting on no particular feeling. This may be called intellectual [118] contentment. Sensuous contentment (improperly so called) which rests on the satisfaction of inclinations, however refined they may be, can never be adequate to that which is conceived under contentment. For inclinations vary; they grow with the indulgence we allow them, and they leave behind a greater void than the one we intended to fill. They are consequently always burdensome to a rational being, and, though he cannot put them aside, they nevertheless elicit from him the wish to be free of them. Even an inclination to do that which accords with duty (e.g., to do beneficent acts) can at most facilitate the effectiveness of moral maxims but not produce any such maxims. For in such maxims, everything must be directed to the thought of the law as the motive if the action is to contain not mere legality but also morality. Inclination, be it good-natured or otherwise, is blind and slavish; reason, when it is a question of morality, must not play the part of mere guardian of the inclinations, but, without regard to them, as pure practical reason it must care for its own interest to the exclusion of all else. Even the feeling of sympathy and warmhearted fellow-feeling, when preceding the consideration of what is duty and serving as a determining ground, is burdensome even to right-thinking persons, confusing their considered maxims and creating the wish to be free from them and subject only to law-giving reason.

Thus we can understand how the consciousness of this capacity of a pure practical reason through a deed (virtue) can produce a consciousness of mastery over inclinations and thus of independence from them and, from the discontentment which always accompanies them, bring forth a negative satisfaction with one's condition, i.e., contentment, whose source is contentment with one's own person. Freedom itself thus becomes in this indirect way capable of being enjoyed. This cannot be called happiness, since it does not depend upon a positive participation of feeling; nor can it be called bliss, because it does not include complete independence from inclinations and desires. It does nevertheless resemble the latter so far at least as the determination of the will which it involves can be held to be free from their influence, and thus, at least in its origin, it is analogous to the self-sufficiency which can be ascribed only to the Supreme Being.

From this solution of the antinomy of practical pure [119] reason, it follows that in practical principles a natural and necessary connection between the consciousness of morality and the expectation of proportionate happiness as its consequence may be thought at least possible, though it is by no means known or understood. On the other hand, it is seen that principles for the pursuit of happiness cannot possibly produce morality and there therefore the supreme good (as the first condition of the highest good) is morality; and that happiness, though it indeed constitutes the second element of the highest good, does so only as the morally conditioned but necessary consequence of the former. Only with this subordination is the highest good the entire object of pure practical reason, which pure practical reason must necessarily think as possible be-

cause reason commands us to contribute everything possible
to its realization. But the possibility of such a connection of the
conditioned with its condition belongs wholly to the supersensible relations of things and cannot be given under the laws
of the world of sense, even though the practical consequence
of this Idea, i.e., the actions which are devoted to realizing the
highest good, do belong to this world. Therefore, we shall seek
to establish the grounds of that possibility primarily with respect to what is immediately in our power, and secondarily in
that which is beyond our power but which reason holds out to
us as the supplement to our impotence to [realize] the possibility of the highest good, which is necessary according to practical principles.

III. ON THE PRIMACY OF PURE PRACTICAL REASON IN ITS ASSOCIATION WITH SPECULATIVE REASON

By primacy between two or more things connected by reason, I understand the prerogative of one by virtue of which it is
the prime ground of determination of the combination with the
others. In a narrower practical sense it refers to the prerogative
of the interest of one so far as the interest of the others is subor-
dinated to it and it is not itself inferior to any other. To every faculty of the mind an interest can be ascribed, i.e., a principle
which contains the condition under which alone its exercise is
advanced. Reason, as the faculty of principles, determines the
interest of all the powers of the mind and its own. The in- [120]
terest of its speculative use consists in the knowledge of objects
up to the highest a priori principles; that of its practical employment lies in the determination of the will with respect to
the final and perfect end. That which is needed in general for
the possibility of any employment of reason, i.e., that its principles and assertions not contradict one another, is not a part of
its interest but is rather the condition of having any reason at all;
only its extension, and not the mere agreement with itself, is
reckoned as its interest.

If practical reason may not assume and think as given anything further than what speculative reason affords from its own insight, the latter has primacy. But suppose that the former has for itself original a priori principles with which certain theoretical positions are inseparably bound but which are beyond any possible insight of speculative reason (although not contradictory to it). Then the question is: Which interest is superior? It is not a question of which must yield, for one does not necessarily conflict with the other. It is a question of whether speculative reason, which knows nothing of that which practical reason offers for its acceptance, must take up these principles and seek to integrate them, even though they transcend it, with its own concepts, as a foreign possession handed over to it; or whether it is justified in stubbornly following its own isolated interest, rejecting, according to the canon of Epicurus, everything as an empty sophism which does not certify its objective reality by manifest examples from experience, doing so however much of it is interwoven with the interest of the practical (pure) use of reason and however far removed from contradicting the theoretical, merely because it infringes upon the interest of speculative reason by removing the bounds which the latter has set itself, opening it to every nonsense and delusion of the imagination.

In fact, so long as practical reason is pathologically conditioned, i.e., as merely regulating the interest of the inclinations by the sensuous principle of happiness, this demand [that theoretical reason should yield primacy to practical reason] could not be made on speculative reason. Mohammed's paradise or the fusion with the deity of the theosophists and mystics, according to the taste of each, would press their monstro- [121] sities on reason, and it would be as well to have no reason at all as to surrender it in such a manner to all sorts of dreams. But if pure reason of itself can be and really is practical, as the consciousness of the moral law shows it to be, it is only one and the same reason which judges a priori by principles, whether for theoretical or for practical purposes. Then it is clear that, if its capacity in the former is not sufficient to establish certain propositions positively (which however do not contradict it), it

must assume these propositions just as soon as they are sufficiently certified as belonging imprescriptibly to the practical
interest of pure reason. It must assume them indeed as something offered from the outside and not grown in its own soil,
and it must seek to compare and connect them with everything
which it has in its power as speculative reason. It must remember that they are not its own insights but extensions of its
use in some other respect, viz., the practical; and that this is not
in the least opposed to its interest, which lies in the restriction
of speculative folly.

Thus in the combination of pure speculative with pure practical reason in one cognition, the latter has primacy, provided
that this combination is not contingent and arbitrary but a
priori, based on reason itself and thus necessary. Without this
subordination, a conflict of reason with itself would arise, since
if the speculative and the practical reason were arranged
merely side by side (co-ordinated), the first would close its
borders and admit into its domain nothing from the latter,
while the latter would extend its boundaries over everything
and, when its needs required, would seek to comprehend the
former within them. Nor could we reverse the order and expect
practical reason to submit to speculative reason, because every
interest is ultimately practical, even that of speculative reason
being only conditional and reaching perfection only in practical use.

IV. THE IMMORTALITY OF THE SOUL AS A POSTULATE OF PURE PRACTICAL REASON

The achievement of the highest good in the world is [122]
the necessary object of a will determinable by moral law. In
such a will, however, the complete fitness of dispositions to the
moral law is the supreme condition of the highest good. This
fitness, therefore, must be just as possible as its object, because
it is contained in the command that requires us to promote the
latter. But the perfect fit of the will to moral law is holiness,
which is a perfection of which no rational being in the world of

sense is at any time capable. But since it is required as practically necessary, it can be found only in an endless progress to that perfect fitness; on principles of pure practical reason, it is necessary to assume such a practical progress as the real object of our will.

This infinite progress is possible, however, only under the presupposition of an infinitely enduring existence and personality of the same rational being; this is called the immortality of the soul. Thus the highest good is practically possible only on the supposition of the immortality of the soul, and the latter, as inseparably bound to the moral law, is a postulate of pure practical reason. By a postulate of pure practical reason, I understand a theoretical proposition which is not as such demonstrable, but which is an inseparable corollary of an a priori unconditionally valid practical law.

The thesis of the moral destiny of our nature, that it is only in an infinite progress that it can attain perfect fitness to moral law, is of the greatest use, not merely for the present purpose of supplementing the impotence of speculative reason, but also with respect to religion. Without it, either the moral law is completely degraded from its holiness, by being made out as lenient (indulgent) and thus compliant to our convenience, or its call and its demands are strained to an unattainable destination, i.e., a hoped-for complete attainment of holiness of will, and are lost in fanatical theosophical dreams which [123] completely contradict our knowledge of ourselves. In either case, we are hindered in the unceasing striving toward exact and steadfast obedience to a command of reason which is stern, unindulgent, truly commanding, really and not just ideally possible.

Only endless progress from lower to higher stages of moral perfection is possible to a rational but finite being. The Infinite Being, to whom the temporal condition is nothing, sees in this series, which is for us without end, a whole comfortable to moral law; holiness, which His law inexorably commands in order to be true to His justice in the share He assigns to each in the highest good, is to be found in a single intellectual intuition of the existence of rational beings. All that can be granted to a creature with respect to hope for this share is consciousness of his tried character. And on the basis of his previous progress from the worse to the morally better, and of the immutability of disposition which thus becomes known to him, he may hope for a further uninterrupted continuance of this progress, however long his existence may last, even beyond this life.* But he cannot hope here or at any foreseeable point of his future existence to be fully adequate to God's will, without indulgence or remission which would not harmonize with justice. [124] This he can do only in the infinity of his duration which God alone can survey.

V. THE EXISTENCE OF GOD AS A POSTULATE OF PURE PRACTICAL REASON

The moral law led, in the foregoing analysis, to a practical task which is assigned solely by pure reason and without any concurrence of sensuous drives. It is the task of perfecting the first and principal part of the highest good, viz., morality; since this task can be executed only in eternity, it led to the postulate of immortality. The same law must also lead us to affirm the

---

*The conviction of the immutability of character in progress toward the good may appear to be impossible for a creature. For this reason, Christian doctrine lets it derive from the same Spirit which works sanctification, i.e., this firm disposition and therewith the consciousness of steadfastness in moral progress. But naturally one who is conscious of having persisted, from legitimate moral motives, to the end of a long life in a progress to the better may very well have the comforting hope, though not the certainty, that he will be steadfast in these principles in an existence continuing beyond this life. Though he can never be justified in his own eyes either here or in the hoped-for increase of natural perfection together with an increase of his duties, nevertheless in this progress toward a goal infinitely remote (a progress which in God's sight is regarded as equivalent to possession) he can have prospect of a blessed future. For "blessed" is the word which reason uses to designate perfect well-being independent of all contingent causes in the world. Like holiness, it is an Idea which can be contained only in an infinite progress and its totality and thus is never fully reached by any creature.

possibility of the second element of the highest good, i.e., happiness proportional to that morality; it must do so just as disinterestedly as heretofore, by a purely impartial reason. This it can do on the supposition of the existence of a cause adequate to this effect. It must postulate the existence of God as necessarily belonging to the possibility of the highest good (the object of our will which is necessarily connected with the moral legislation of pure reason). We proceed to exhibit this connection in a convincing manner.

Happiness is the condition of a rational being in the world, in whose whole existence everything goes according to wish and will. It thus rests on the harmony of nature with his whole end and with the essential determining ground of his will. But the moral law as a law of freedom commands through motives wholly independent of nature and of its harmony with our faculty of desire (as drives). Still, the acting rational being in the world is not at the same time the cause of the world and of nature itself. Hence there is not the slightest ground in the moral law for a necessary connection between the morality and proportionate happiness of a being who belongs to the world as one of its parts and is thus dependent on it. Not being nature's cause, his will cannot by its own strength bring nature, as it touches on his happiness, into perfect harmony with his practical principles. Nevertheless, in the practical task of [125] pure reason, i.e., in the necessary endeavor after the highest good, such a connection is postulated as necessary: we *ought to* seek to further the highest good (which therefore must be at least possible). Therefore also the existence is postulated of a cause of the whole of nature, itself distinct from nature, which contains the ground of the exact coincidence of happiness with morality. This supreme cause, however, must contain the ground of the agreement of nature not merely with a law of the will of rational beings but with the representation of this law so far as they make it the supreme motive of the will. Thus it contains the ground of the agreement of nature not merely with actions moral in their form but also with their morality as the motives to such actions, i.e., with their moral disposition. Therefore, the highest good is possible in the world only on

the supposition of a supreme cause of nature which has a causality corresponding to the moral disposition. Now a being capable of actions by the representation of laws is an intelligence (a
rational being), and the causality of such a being according to
this representation of laws is his will. Therefore, the supreme
cause of nature, in so far as it must be presupposed for the
highest good, is a being which is the cause (and consequently
the author) of nature through understanding and will, i.e.,
God. As a consequence, the postulate of the possibility of a
highest derivative good (the best world) is at the same time the
postulate of the reality of a highest original good, namely, the
postulate of the existence of God. Now it was our duty to promote the highest good; and it is not merely our privilege but a
necessity connected with duty as a requisite to presuppose the
possibility of this highest good. This presupposition is made
only under the condition of the existence of God, and this condition inseparably connects this supposition with duty. Therefore, it is morally necessary to assume the existence of God.

It is well to notice here that this moral necessity is subjective,
i.e., a need, and not objective, i.e., duty itself. For there cannot
be any duty to assume the existence of a thing, because such a
supposition concerns only the theoretical use of reason. It is
also not to be understood that the assumption of the existence
of God is necessary as a ground of all obligation in general (for
this rests, as has been fully shown, solely on the auto- [126]
nomy of reason itself). All that here belongs to duty is the endeavor to produce and to further the highest good in the world,
the possibility of which may thus be postulated though our reason cannot conceive it except by presupposing a Highest Intelligence. To assume its existence is thus connected with the
consciousness of our duty, though this assumption itself belongs to the realm of theoretical reason. Considered only in reference to the latter, it is an hypothesis, i.e., a ground of explanation. But in reference to the comprehensibility of an object (the
highest good) placed before us by the moral law, and thus as a
practical need, it can be called *faith* and even pure *rational*

faith, because pure reason alone (by its theoretical as well as practical employment) is the source from which it springs.

From this deduction it now becomes clear why the Greek schools could never succeed in solving their problem of the practical possibility of the highest good. It was because they made the rule of the use which the human will makes of its freedom the sole and self-sufficient ground of its possibility, thinking that they had no need of the existence of God for this purpose. They were certainly correct in establishing the principle of morals by itself, independently of this postulate and merely from the relation of reason to the will, thus making the principle of morality the *supreme* practical condition of the highest good; but this principle was not the *entire* condition of its possibility. The Epicureans had indeed raised a wholly false principle of morality, i.e., that of happiness, into the supreme one, and for law had substituted a maxim of free choice of each according to his inclination. But they proceeded consistently enough, in that they degraded their highest good in proportion to the baseness of their principle and expected no greater happiness than that which could be attained through human prudence (wherein both temperance and the moderation of inclinations belong), though everyone knows prudence to be scarce enough and to produce diverse results according to circumstances, not to mention the exceptions which their maxims continually had to admit and which made them worthless as laws. The Stoics, on the other hand, had chosen their supreme practical principle, virtue, quite correctly as the condition of the highest good. But as they imagined the degree of virtue which is required for its pure law as completely [127] attainable in this life, they not only exaggerated the moral capacity of man, under the name of "sage," beyond all the limits of his nature, making it into something which is contradicted by all our knowledge of men; they also refused to accept the second component of the highest good, i.e., happiness, as a special object of human desire. Rather, they made their sage, like a god in the consciousness of the excellence of his person,

wholly independent of nature (as regards his own contentment), exposing him to the evils of life but not subjecting him
to them. (They also represented him as free from everything
morally evil.) Thus they really left out of the highest good the
second element (personal happiness), since they placed the
highest good only in acting and in contentment with one's own
personal worth, including it in the consciousness of moral
character. But the voice of their own nature could have sufficiently refuted this.

The doctrine of Christianity* even when not regarded as a

*The view is commonly held that the Christian precept of morals has no ad-
vantage over the moral concept of the Stoics in respect to its purity; but the difference between them is nevertheless obvious. The Stoic system makes the
consciousness of strength of mind the pivot around which all moral dispositions should turn; and, if the followers of this system spoke of duties and even
defined them accurately, they nevertheless placed the drives and the real motive of the will in an elevation of character above the base drives of the senses
which have their power only through weakness of the mind. Virtue was, therefore, for them a certain heroism of the sage who, raising himself above the animal nature of man, was sufficient to himself, subject to no temptation to transgress the moral law, and elevated above duties though he propounded duties
to others. But all this they could not have done had they conceived this law in
the same purity and rigor as does the precept of the Gospel. If I understand by
Idea a perfection to which the senses can give nothing adequate, moral Ideas
are not transcendent, i.e., of such a kind that we cannot even sufficiently define
the concept or of which we are uncertain whether there is a corresponding object (as are the Ideas of speculative reason); rather, they serve as models of
practical perfection, as an indispensable rule of moral conduct, and as a standard for comparison. If I now regard Christian morals from their philosophical
side, it appears in comparison with the ideas of the Greek schools as follows:
the ideas of the Cynics, Epicureans, Stoics, and Christians are, respectively, the
simplicity of nature, prudence, wisdom, and holiness. In respect to the way
they achieve them, the Greek schools differ in that the Cynics found common
sense sufficient, while the others found it in the path of science, and thus all
held it to lie in the use of man's natural powers. Christian ethics, because it for-
mulated its precept as pure and uncompromising (as befits a moral precept),
destroyed man's confidence of being wholly adequate to it, at least in this life;
but it re-established it by enabling us to hope that, if we act as well as lies in our
power, what is not in our power will come to our aid from another source,
whether we know in what way or not. Aristotle and Plato differed only as to the
origin of our moral concepts.

religious doctrine, gives at this point a concept of the [128] highest good (the Kingdom of God) which is alone sufficient to the strictest demand of practical reason. The moral law is holy (unyielding) and demands holiness of morals, although all moral perfection to which man can attain is only virtue, i.e., a law-abiding disposition resulting from respect for the law and thus implying consciousness of a continuous propensity to transgress it or at least to a defilement, i.e., to an admixture of many spurious (not moral) motives to obedience to the law; consequently, man can achieve only self-esteem combined with humility. And thus with respect to the holiness required by the Christian law, nothing remains to the creature but end-less progress, though for the same reason hope for endless du-ration is justified. The worth of a character completely accor-dant with the moral law is infinite, because all possible happiness in the judgment of a wise and omnipotent dispenser of happiness has no other limitation than the lack of fitness of rational beings to their duty. But the moral law does not of itself promise happiness, for happiness is not, according to concepts of any order of nature, necessarily connected with obedience to the law. Christian ethics supplies this defect of the second in-dispensable component of the highest good by presenting a world wherein reasonable beings single-mindedly devote themselves to the moral law; this is the Kingdom of God, in which nature and morality come into a harmony, which is for-eign to each as such, through a holy Author of the world, who makes possible the derived highest good. The holiness of morals is prescribed to them even in this life as a guide to con-duct, but well-being proportionate to this, which is bliss, is thought of as attainable only in eternity. This is due to [129] the fact that the former must always be the archetype of their conduct in every state, and progressing toward it is even in this life possible and necessary, whereas the latter, under the name of happiness, cannot (as far as our own capacity is concerned) be reached in this life and therefore is made only an object of hope. Nevertheless, the Christian principle of morality is not theological and thus heteronomous, being rather the autonomy of pure practical reason itself, because it does not make the knowledge of God and His will the basis of these laws but makes such knowledge the basis only of succeeding to the highest good on condition of obedience to these laws; it places the real incentive for obedience to the law not in the desired consequences of obedience but in the conception of duty alone, in true observance of which the worthiness to attain the latter alone consists.

In this manner, through the concept of the highest good as the object and final end of pure practical reason, the moral law leads to religion. Religion is the recognition of all duties as divine commands, not as sanctions, i.e., arbitrary and contingent ordinances of a foreign will, but as essential laws of any free will as such. Even as such, they must be regarded as commands of the Supreme Being because we can hope for the highest good (to strive for which is our duty under the moral law) only from a morally perfect (holy and beneficent) and omnipotent will; and, therefore, we can hope to attain it only through harmony with this will. But here again everything remains disinterested and based only on duty, without being based on fear or hope as drives, which, if they became principles, would destroy the entire moral worth of the actions. The moral law commands us to make the highest possible good in a world the final object of all our conduct. This I cannot hope to effect except through the agreement of my will with that of a holy and beneficent Author of the world. And although my own happiness is included in the concept of the highest good as a whole wherein the greatest happiness is thought of as connected in exact proportion to the greatest degree of moral perfection pos- [130] sible to creatures, still it is not happiness but the moral law (which, in fact, sternly places restricting conditions upon my boundless longing for happiness) which is proved to be the ground determining the will to further the highest good.

Therefore, morals is not really the doctrine of how to make ourselves happy but of how we are to be *worthy* of happiness. Only if religion is added to it can the hope arise of someday participating in happiness in proportion as we endeavored not to be unworthy of it.

One is worthy of possessing a thing or a state when his possession is harmonious with the highest good. We can easily see now that all worthiness is a matter of moral conduct, because this constitutes the condition of everything else (which belongs to one's state) in the concept of the highest good, i.e., participation in happiness. From this it follows that one must never consider morals itself as a doctrine of happiness, i.e., as an instruction in how to acquire happiness. For morals has to do only with the rational condition (*conditio sine qua non*) of happiness and not with means of achieving it. But when morals (which imposes only duties instead of providing rules for selfish wishes) is completely expounded, and a moral wish has been awakened to promote the highest good (to bring the Kingdom of God to us), which is a wish based on law and one to which no selfish mind could have aspired, and when for the sake of this wish the step to religion has been taken—then only can ethics be called a doctrine of happiness, because the *hope* for it first arises with religion.

From this it can also be seen that, if we inquire into God's final end in creating the world, we must name not the happiness of rational beings in the world but the highest good, which adds a further condition to the wish of rational beings to be happy, viz., the condition of being worthy of happiness, which is the morality of these beings, for this alone contains the standard by which they can hope to participate in happiness at the hand of a wise creator. For since wisdom, theoretically regarded, means the knowledge of the highest good and, practically, the conformability of the will to the highest good, [131] one cannot ascribe to a supreme independent wisdom an end based merely on benevolence. For we cannot conceive the action of this benevolence (with respect to the happiness of rational beings) except as conformable to the restrictive conditions of harmony with the holiness* of His will as the highest origi-

*Incidentally, and in order to make the peculiarity of this concept clear, I make the following remark. Although we ascribe various attributes to God, whose quality we find suitable also to creatures (e.g., power, knowledge, presence, goodness, etc.), which in God are present in a higher degree under such names as omnipotence, omniscience, omnipresence, and perfect goodness,

nal good. Then perhaps those who have placed the end of creation in the glory of God, provided this is not thought of
anthropomorphically as an inclination to be esteemed, have
found the best term. For nothing glorifies God more than what
is the most estimable thing in the world, namely, reverence for
His command, the observance of sacred duty which His law
imposes on us, when there is added to this His glorious plan of
crowning such an excellent order with corresponding happiness. If the latter, to speak in human terms, makes Him worthy
of love, by the former He is an object of adoration. Human
beings can win love by doing good, but by this alone even they
never win respect; the greatest well-doing does them honor
only by being exercised according to [their] worthiness.

It follows of itself that, in the order of ends, man (and every
rational being) is an end in himself, i.e., he is never to be used
merely as a means for someone (even for God) without at the
same time being himself an end, and that humanity in our person must itself be holy to us, because man is subject to the
moral law and therefore subject to that which is of itself holy,
and it is only on account of this and in agreement with [132]
this that anything can be called holy. For this moral law is
founded on the autonomy of his will as a free will, which by its
universal laws must necessarily be able to agree with that to
which he ought to subject himself.

VI. ON THE POSTULATES OF PURE PRACTICAL
REASON IN GENERAL

The postulates of pure practical reason all proceed from the
principle of morality, which is not a postulate but a law by

---

etc., there are three which exclusively and without qualification of magnitude
are ascribed to God, and they are all moral. He is the only holy, the only
blessed, and the only wise being, because these concepts of themselves imply
unlimitedness. By the arrangement of these He is thus the holy lawgiver (and
creator), the beneficent ruler (and sustainer), and the just judge. These three
attributes contain everything whereby God is the object of religion, and in conformity to them the metaphysical perfections of themselves arise in reason.

which reason directly determines the will. This will, by the fact that it is so determined, as a pure will requires these necessary conditions for obedience to its precept. These postulates are not theoretical dogmas but presuppositions of necessarily practical import; thus, while they do not extend speculative knowledge, they give objective reality to the Ideas of speculative reason *in general* (by means of their relation to the practical sphere), and they justify speculative reason in holding to concepts even the possibility of which it could not otherwise venture to affirm.

These postulates are those of immortality, of freedom affirmatively regarded (as the causality of a being so far as he belongs to the intelligible world), and of the existence of God. The first derives from the practically necessary condition of a duration adequate to the perfect fulfilment of the moral law. The second comes from the necessary presupposition of independence from the world of sense and of the capacity of determining man's will by the law of an intelligible world, i.e., the law of freedom itself; the third arises from the necessary condition of such an intelligible world by which it may be the highest good, through the presupposition of the highest independent good, i.e., the existence of God.

The prospect of the highest good, necessary through respect for the moral law and the consequent supposition of its objective reality, thus leads through postulates of practical reason to concepts which speculative reason only exhibited as problems which it could not solve. It leads first to the problem of immortality, in the solution of which speculative reason [133] could only commit paralogisms, because the marks of permanence, by which the psychological concept of an ultimate subject necessarily ascribed to the soul in self-consciousness, were lacking though they were needed to complete the real conception of a substance. Practical reason, through the postulates of fitness to the moral law in the highest good as the whole end of practical reason, consigns to this subject the requisite duration. Secondly, it leads to the concept which speculative reason contained only as an antinomy, and the solution of which it could base only on a problematical, though thinkable, concept whose objective reality was not provable or determinable by speculative reason. This is the cosmological Idea of an intelligible world and the consciousness of our existence in it. It leads to this by means of the postulate of freedom (the reality of which practical reason exhibits in the moral law, at the same time exhibiting the law of an intelligible world, which speculative reason could only indicate but whose concept it could not define). Thirdly, it gives significance to what speculative reason could indeed think but had to leave indeterminate as a mere transcendental *Ideal*, i.e., to the theological concept of the First Being. This significance is given in a practical point of view, i.e., as a condition of the possibility of the object of a will determined by that law. It is that of a supreme principle of the highest good in an intelligible world having sovereign power in it by means of a moral legislation.

Is our knowledge really widened in such a way by pure practical reason, and is that which was transcendent for speculative reason immanent in practical reason? Certainly, but only from a practical point of view. For we thereby know neither the nature of our soul, nor the intelligible world, nor the Supreme Being as they are in themselves, but have only united the concepts of them in a practical concept of the highest good as the object of our will and have done so entirely a priori through pure reason. We have so united them only by means of the moral law and merely in relation to it, with respect to the object which it commands. But how freedom is possible, and how we should think theoretically and positively of this type of causality, is not thereby discovered. All that is comprehended is that such a causality is postulated through the moral law and for its sake. It is the same with the remaining Ideas, whose possibility cannot be fathomed by human understanding, though no [134] sophistry will ever wrest from the conviction of even the most ordinary man an admission that they are not true.

VII. HOW IS IT POSSIBLE TO CONCEIVE OF EXTENDING PURE REASON IN A PRACTICAL RESPECT WITHOUT THEREBY EXTENDING ITS KNOWLEDGE AS SPECULATIVE?

In order not to be too abstract, we shall answer this question by direct application to the present case. In order to extend pure knowledge practically, an a priori purpose must be given, i.e., an end as an object (of the will) which, independently of all theoretical principles, is thought of as practically necessary through a categorical imperative directly determining the will. In this case, the object is the highest good; but it is not possible unless three theoretical concepts are presupposed: freedom, immortality, and God. Since they are pure concepts of reason, however, no corresponding intuition can be given and consequently no objective reality for them can be found in a theoretical way. Therefore, through the practical law, which requires the existence of the highest good possible in the world, there is postulated the possibility of those objects of pure speculative reason whose objective reality could not be assured by speculative reason. By this, then, the theoretical knowledge of pure reason does obtain an accession, but it consists only in this — that those concepts which for it are otherwise problematical (merely thinkable) are now described assertorically as actually having objects, because practical reason inexorably requires the existence of these objects for the possibility of its practically and absolutely necessary object, the highest good. Theoretical reason is, therefore, justified in assuming them.

This extension of theoretical reason, however, is not an extension of speculation. That is, a positive use cannot be made of those objects for theoretical purposes. For nothing more has here been accomplished by practical reason than to show that those concepts are real and actually have (possible) objects, but no intuitions of them are thereby given (and indeed none can be demanded), and thus no synthetic proposition is made possible by conceding their reality. Consequently, this disclosure does not in the least help us in a speculative respect, [135] but it does aid us with reference to the practical use of pure rea-

son in extending our knowledge in this field. The three aforementioned Ideas of speculative reason are not themselves cognitions; they are, nevertheless, transcendent thoughts in which
there is nothing impossible. Now through an apodictic practical law, as necessary conditions of the possibility of that which
this law requires to be made an object, they acquire objective
reality. That is to say, they show by this that they have objects,
but we cannot indicate how their concept refers to an object;
this, too, is not yet knowledge of these objects, for we can
thereby neither make synthetic judgments about them nor
theoretically determine their application. Consequently, we
can make no theoretical rational use of them, and it is in this
that all speculative knowledge of reason actually consists. Nevertheless, theoretical knowledge not of these objects but of
reason in general was extended so far that, by the practical postulates, objects were given to those Ideas, and a merely problematical thought thereby obtained objective reality. It was
therefore no extension of knowledge of given supersensible
objects, but still an extension of theoretical reason and of its
knowledge with respect to the supersensible in general, inasmuch as knowledge is compelled to concede that there are
such objects without more exactly defining them, and thus
without being able to extend this knowledge of objects given to
it only on practical grounds and only for practical use. For this
accession, pure theoretical reason has thus to thank its pure
practical faculty, for all these Ideas are to it transcendent and
without objects. Here they become immanent and constitutive,
since they are the grounds of the possibility of realizing the
necessary object of pure practical reason (the highest good);
otherwise they are transcendent and merely regulative principles of speculative reason, which is charged with the task not of
assuming a new object beyond experience but only of approaching perfection in its employment within experience.
Once in possession of this accession, for the security of its
practical employment it will set to work as speculative reason
with these Ideas in a negative manner, i.e., not broadening but
purifying, in order to ward off anthropomorphism as the source

of superstition (apparent extension of those concepts [136] through alleged experience) and fanaticism which promises such an extension through supersensuous intuition or feelings. Both of these are obstacles to the practical use of pure reason, and the safeguard against them certainly belongs in the extension of our knowledge in a practical direction, without contradicting the admission that reason has not gained anything at all in a speculative direction.

To each employment of reason with respect to objects, pure concepts of the understanding (categories) are required, for without them no object can be thought. These can be applied to the theoretical employment of reason, i.e., to that kind of knowledge only in case intuition (which is always sensible) is supplied as their basis in order that through it an object of possible experience may be represented. Ideas of reason, which cannot be given in any experience, are that which I would have to think here through categories in order to know the object. But here we have not to do with theoretical knowledge of objects of these Ideas but only with whether they do have objects or not. This reality is supplied by pure practical reason, and in relation to them theoretical reason has nothing further to do than merely to think those objects by means of categories. This occurs very well, as we have elsewhere clearly shown, without need of intuition (either sensible or supersensible), because the categories have their seat and origin in pure understanding as the sole faculty of thinking independent of and prior to any intuition; and they always signify only an object in general, *in whatever way it may be given to us.* Now no object in intuition can be given to the categories so far as they are to be applied to these Ideas; but that such an object really exists and that here the category as a mere form of thought is not empty but has significance — this is sufficiently certified by an object which practical reason indubitably presents in the concept of the highest good, namely, by the reality of the concepts that are required for the possibility of the highest good. But even the least extension of our knowledge by theoretical principles is not effected by this accession.

When these Ideas of God, an intelligible world (the [137] Kingdom of God), and immortality are further defined with predicates derived from our own nature, such definition cannot be regarded as making pure rational Ideas sensuous (which is equivalent to anthropomorphism) or as being transcendent knowledge of supersensible objects. For these predicates are nothing else than understanding and will, in their contrasting relationship to one another, as they must be thought in the moral law, i.e., as they must be thought only in so far as a pure practical use is made of them. Everything else which pertains psychologically to these concepts, i.e., everything known only as we empirically observe these faculties of ours in their exercise, is therefore removed from them. For example, it is disregarded that human understanding is discursive, that its representations are thoughts and not intuitions, that intuitions succeed each other in time, that the human will is always dependent for its contentment upon the existence of its object, etc., none of which can be the case with the Highest Being. Thus there remains nothing more in the concepts by which we think a pure rational being than what is directly required for thinking a moral law. There remains, then, a knowledge of God, but only in a practical context. And if we essay to extend it to a theoretical context, we get a divine understanding which does not think but intuits and a will which is directed to objects on the existence of which its contentment does not in the least depend. (I need not even mention the transcendental predicates, e.g., of magnitude of existence, duration, which is not in time even though this is the only means by which we can think of the magnitude of existence.) All of them are just qualities of which we can form no concept adequate to knowledge of objects. We learn in this way that they can never be used in a *theory* of supersensible beings and that therefore from the theoretical aspect they can never support speculative knowledge, their use being restricted solely to the practice of the moral law.

The latter is so obvious and can be so clearly proved by fact that one can confidently challenge all pretended natural theologians (a curious name)* to cite one single definitive [138] attribute (beyond the merely ontological predicates) of their object (say, of the understanding or the will), of which one could not irrefutably show that, when everything anthropomorphic is removed, only the word remains, without there being any possibility of connecting the least concept with it by which an extension of theoretical knowledge might be expected. But as to the practical, there still remains to us, of the attributes of an understanding and a will, the concept of a relation which is given objective reality by the practical law, which a priori determines precisely this relation of the understanding to the will. If this is once done, reality is given to the concept of the object of a morally determined will (i.e., to the highest good), and therewith the conditions of its possibility, the Ideas of God, freedom, and immortality. But this reality is still given only with reference to the practice of the moral law and not for any speculative use.

After this reminder it is easy to find the answer to the important question: Is the concept of God a concept belonging to physics (and thus also to metaphysics, as this only contains the pure a priori principles of physics in their universal import) or a concept belonging to morals? To have recourse to God as the Author of all things, in explaining the arrangements of nature and their changes is at any rate not a physical explanation but a complete confession that one has come to the end of his philosophy, since he is compelled to assume something of which in itself he otherwise has no concept in order to conceive of the possibility of something he sees before his very eyes. It is im-

---

*"Learning" is a word properly applied only to the historical sciences. Consequently, only the teacher of revealed theology can be called a theologian.[1] But if one wishes to call someone who is in possession of the rational sciences (mathematics and philosophy) a "learned" man, even though this would contradict the meaning of the word (which attributes to learning only that which must be *taught* and thus what one cannot of himself discover by reason), the philosopher with his knowledge of God as a positive science would certainly cut too poor a figure to deserve the name of a "learned" man.

[1] *Gottesgelehrter*, lit., "one learned about God."

possible by means of metaphysics to progress from knowledge of this world to concepts of God and a proof of his existence through cogent inferences, because we should have to know *this* world as the most perfect possible whole, and to this end we should have to know all possible worlds in order to compare it to them — in short, we should have to be omniscient — in order to say that it is possible only through a God, [139] however we understand this concept. To know completely the existence of this Being from mere concepts is absolutely impossible, for any existential proposition which asserts the existence of a being of which I have a concept is a synthetic proposition; that is, it is such that I must go beyond the concept and assert more than was thought in it, namely, that outside the understanding there is an object corresponding to the concept within the understanding. This assertion obviously cannot be reached by any inference.

Thus there remains to reason only one single procedure by which it can arrive at this knowledge: as pure reason it must determine its object by starting from the supreme principle of its pure practical use (since this is directed in every case only to the *existence* of something as a consequence of reason). In the unavoidable task of directing the will to the highest good, there is not only shown the necessity of assuming such a First Being in relation to the possibility of this good in the world but — which is more remarkable — there is also shown an exactly defined concept of this Being, something completely lacking in the progress of reason in the path of nature. Since we know only a small part of this world and even less can compare it with all possible worlds, we can very well infer from its order, design, and magnitude to a wise, beneficent, and powerful Author of it, but not that He is all-knowing, all-good, and all-powerful. It may even be conceded that one is privileged to supplement this unavoidable lack by a permissible and wholly reasonable hypothesis to the effect that since wisdom, beneficence, etc., are displayed in all the parts offered to our more exact knowledge, it will be the same with all the rest, and that therefore it is reasonable to ascribe every possible perfection to the Author of the world. But these are not inferences in which we can pride ourselves on our insight; they are only liberties which may be allowed but which need further recommendation before they can be used. On the path of empirical inquiry (physics), the concept of God always remains a concept of the perfection of the First Being which is not accurately enough defined to be held suitable to the concept of Deity. (And with metaphysics in its transcendental part nothing at all can be accomplished.)

When I try now to test this concept by reference to the [140] object of practical reason, I find that the moral principle admits this concept as possible only under the presupposition of an Author of the world having the highest perfection. This Being must be omniscient, in order to be able to know my conduct even to the most intimate parts of my disposition in all possible cases and in the entire future. In order to allot fitting consequences to it, He must be omnipotent, and similarly omnipresent, eternal, etc. Thus the moral law, by the concept of the highest good as the object of pure practical reason, defines the concept of the First Being as that of a Supreme Being. This cannot be accomplished by the physical (and its higher development, the metaphysical) or, consequently, by any speculative procedure of reason. Therefore, the concept of God is one which belongs originally not to physics, i.e., to speculative reason, but to morals. The same may be said of the other concepts of reason which we have previously treated as postulates of reason in its practical use.

In the history of Greek philosophy before Anaxagoras there is no definite trace of a pure rational theology. The reason for this is not that the earlier philosophers lacked the understanding and insight to raise themselves to it by way of speculation, at least with the aid of a very reasonable hypothesis. For what could be easier than the thought which of itself occurs to everyone, to assume a single rational world-cause possessing every perfection instead of several different causes or indeterminate degrees of perfection? But the evils in the world appeared to them to be too important an objection for them to hold such a hypothesis to be justified. Thus they showed their understanding and insight precisely in that they did not permit themselves this hypothesis but rather sought among natural causes to see whether they could find among them the character and competence required for the primordial beings. But when this acute people had progressed far enough in their inquiries to deal philosophically even with moral subjects, about which other peoples had never done more than talk, they found for the first time a new need, a practical need which gave them the definite concept of the First Being. In this, speculative reason was only a spectator, or at best it had the merit of embellishing a concept which did not grow on its own ground and of promoting it with a series of confirmations drawn from the observation of [141] nature (which now for the first time came into play). It did not have to strengthen the authority of this concept (which was already established) but only to make a show with a pretended theoretical insight of reason.

By this reminder, the reader of the *Critique of Pure* (speculative) *Reason* will be convinced how much that laborious deduction of the categories was needed for theology and morals and how fruitful it was for them. For if we place them in the pure understanding, it is only by this deduction that we are prevented from holding them, with Plato, to be inborn and from erecting on them transcendent presumptions and theories of the supersensible, the end of which we cannot see, making theology merely a magic lantern of phantoms. And if, on the other hand, they are held to be acquired, this deduction prevents us from limiting their use, with Epicurus, to sensible objects and motives even when their use is practical. But the *Critique* showed in that deduction, first, that they are not of empirical origin but have their source and place a priori in pure understanding; and, second, that since they are related to objects in general independently of an intuition of them, they produce theoretical knowledge only by application to empirical objects. Yet it showed, furthermore, that they enable us to think definite thoughts about the supersensible when applied to an object given by pure practical reason, but only so far as this object is defined by predicates which necessarily belong to a pure practical purpose and its possibility, as given a priori. Speculative restriction and practical extension of pure reason bring pure reason into that relation of balance, wherein reason as such can be suitably used; and this example proves better than any other that the path to wisdom, if it is assured and not made impassable or misleading, must for us men unavoidably pass through science. But we can be sure that it leads to that goal only after the completion of the science.

VIII. ON ASSENT ARISING FROM A NEED OF PURE REASON

A need of pure reason in its speculative use leads [142] only to hypotheses; that of pure practical reason, to postulates. For, in the first case, I may ascend from the result as far as I wish in the series of conditions, and I shall need an ultimate ground not in order to give objective reality to the result (e.g., the causal connection of things and changes in the world) but only in order completely to satisfy my inquiring reason with respect to them. Thus before me I see order and design in nature, and I do not need to go over to speculation in order to assure myself of their reality, though in order to explain them I need to presuppose a Deity as their cause; but since an inference from an effect to a definite cause, especially to one so exactly and perfectly defined as we have to think God to be, is always uncertain and fallible, such a presupposition cannot be brought to a higher degree of certainty than the acknowledgement that it is the most reasonable opinion for us men.*

* But even here we could not allege a need of reason if there were not before us a problematical but inevitable concept of reason, that of an absolutely necessary being. This concept requires to be defined, and, when the tendency to extend [the capacity of reason] is added, it is the objective ground of a need of speculative reason, which is the need to define more accurately the concept of a necessary being which will serve as the ultimate ground of others and thus to characterize this necessary being by a distinctive mark. Without such prior necessary problems there are no needs, at least none of pure reason, the others being needs of inclination.

A need of pure practical reason, on the other hand, is based on a duty to make something (the highest good) the object of my will so as to promote it with all my strength. In doing so, I must presuppose its possibility and also its conditions, which are God, freedom, and immortality; these conditions I am not in a position to prove by my speculative reason, though I cannot disprove them either. This duty is based on an apodictic law, the moral law, which is independent of these presuppositions, and thus needs no further support from theoretical [143] opinions on the inner character of things, on the secret final end of the world order, or on a ruler presiding over it in order to bind us completely to actions unconditionally conformable to the law. The disposition to promote the practically possible highest good is the subjective effect of the law, suitable to and necessary because of it. This subjective effect presupposes that the highest good is possible; otherwise it would be practically impossible to strive for the object of a concept, which, at bottom, would be empty and without an object. Now the aforementioned postulates concern only the physical or metaphysical conditions (that is, those lying in the nature of things) of the possibility of the highest good, though not for the sake of some arbitrary speculative design but only for the sake of a practically necessary end of the pure rational will, which does not here choose but rather obeys an inexorable command of reason. This command of reason has its ground objectively in the character of things as they must be universally judged by pure reason and is not based on inclination, which would by no means justify us in assuming the means to be possible or the object to be real for the sake of that which we wish on merely subjective grounds. This therefore is an absolutely necessary need and justifies its presupposition not merely as an allowable hypothesis but as a practical postulate. Granted that the pure moral law inexorably binds every man as a command (not as a rule of prudence), the righteous man may say: I will that there be a God, that my existence in this world be also an existence in a pure world of the understanding outside the system of natural connections, and finally that my duration be endless. I stand by this and will not give up this belief, for this is the only case where my interest inevitably determines my judgment because I will not yield anything of this interest; I do so without any attention to sophistries, however little I may be able to answer them or oppose them with others more plausible.*

In order to avoid all misinterpretations of the use of [144] such an unusual concept as that of pure practical faith, I may add one more remark. It might almost seem as if this rational faith is here decreed as a command to assume as possible the highest good. But faith that is commanded is an absurdity. If one remembers from the preceding analysis what needs to be presupposed in the concept of the highest good, one will realize that to assume this possibility cannot be commanded, and that no practical disposition to grant it can be demanded, but that speculative reason must admit it without being asked; for no one can hope to affirm that it is impossible of itself that rational beings in the world should at the same time be worthy of

*In the *Deutsches Museum* for February, 1787, there is a dissertation by a very subtle and clear-headed man, the late Wizenmann,[2] whose early death is to be lamented. In this he disputes the right to argue from a need to the objective reality of the object of the need, and he illustrates his point by the example of a man in love, who has fooled himself with an idea of beauty which is merely a chimera of his own brain and who now tries to argue that such an object really exists somewhere. I concede that he is right in all cases where the need is based on inclination, which cannot postulate the existence of its object even for him who is beset by it, which even less contains a demand valid for everyone, and which is therefore a merely subjective ground of wishes. Here we have to do, however, with a need of reason arising from an objective determining ground of the will, i.e., the moral law, which is necessarily binding on every rational being; this, therefore, justifies a priori the presupposition of suitable conditions in nature and makes them inseparable from the complete practical use of reason. It is a duty to realize the highest good as far as it lies within our power to do so; therefore, it must be possible to do so. Consequently, it is unavoidable for every rational being in the world to assume whatever is necessary to its objective possibility. The assumption is as necessary as the moral law, in relation to which alone it is valid.

[2]Thomas Wizenmann (1759–1787), an ally of F. H. Jacobi in his controversy with Mendelssohn about Lessing's Spinozism. On the philosophical issue involved, see xvi, note 13.

happiness in conformity to the moral law and be in possession of happiness proportionate to this worthiness. Now with respect to the first component of the highest good, viz., morality, the moral law merely gives a command, and to doubt the possibility of that component would be the same as to call the moral law itself into question. But with respect to the second component of that object, viz., happiness perfectly proportionate to that worthiness, the assumption of its possibility is not at all in need of a command, for theoretical reason has nothing to say against it. It is only in the way in which we are to think of this harmony of natural laws with laws of freedom that there [145] is anything about which we have a choice, because here theoretical reason does not decide with apodictic certainty, and in this respect there can be a moral interest which turns the scale.

I have said above that in the mere course of nature happiness exactly proportionate to moral worth is not to be expected and is indeed impossible and that therefore the possibility of the highest good from this side cannot be granted except under the presupposition of a moral Author of the world. I intentionally postponed restricting this judgment to the subjective conditions of our reason in order to make use of this restriction only when the manner of the assent had been more precisely defined. In fact, the impossibility mentioned is merely subjective, i.e., our reason finds it impossible to conceive, in the mere course of nature, a connection so exactly proportioned and so thoroughly adapted to an end between natural events which occur according to laws so heterogeneous. But, as with every other purposive thing in nature, it still cannot prove that it is impossible according to universal laws of nature, i.e., show this by objectively sufficient reasons.

But now a determining factor of another kind comes into play to turn the scale in this indecision of speculative reason. The command to further the highest good is objectively grounded (in practical reason), and its possibility itself is likewise objectively grounded (in theoretical reason, which has nothing to say against it). But as to the manner in which we are to think this possibility, reason cannot objectively decide whether it is by universal laws of nature without a wise Author presiding over nature or only on the assumption of such an Author. Now a subjective condition or reason enters which is the only way in which it is theoretically possible for it to conceive of the exact harmony of the realm of nature with the realm of morals as the condition of the possibility of the highest good; and it is the only way which is conducive to morality (which is under an objective law of reason). Since the promotion of the highest good and thus the presupposition of its possibility are objectively necessary (though only as a consequence of practical reason), and since the manner in which we are to think of it as possible is subject to our own choice, in which a free interest of pure practical reason is decisive for the assumption [146] of a wise Author of the world, it follows that the principle which here determines our judgment, while subjectively a need, is the ground of a maxim or moral assent, as a means to promoting that which is objectively (practically) necessary; that is, it is a *faith of pure practical reason*. As a voluntary decision of our judgment to assume that existence and to make it the foundation of further employment of reason, conducing to the moral (commanded) purpose and agreeing moreover with the theoretical need of reason, it is itself not commanded. It rather springs from the moral disposition itself. It can therefore often waver even in the well disposed, but can never fall into unbelief.

IX. OF THE WISE ADAPTATION OF MAN'S COGNITIVE FACULTIES TO HIS PRACTICAL VOCATION

If human nature is called upon to strive for the highest good, the measure of its cognitive faculties and especially their relation to one another must be assumed to be suitable to this end. But the *Critique of Pure* (speculative) *Reason* demonstrates the utter insufficiency of speculative reason to solve the most weighty problems which are presented to it in a way satisfactory to its end; but that *Critique* did not ignore the natural and unmistakable hints of the same reason or the great steps that it can taken in approaching this great goal which is set before it but which it can never of itself reach even with the aid of the greatest knowledge of nature. Thus nature here seems to have provided us only in a stepmotherly fashion with a faculty needed for our end.

Now assuming that it had here indulged our wish and had provided us with that power of insight or enlightenment which we would like to possess or which some erroneously believe they do possess, what would be the consequence so far as we can discern it? In so far as our whole nature was not changed at the same time, the inclinations (which under any condition have the first word) would first strive for their satisfaction and, conjoined with reasonable consideration, for their [147] greatest possible and most lasting satisfaction under the name of happiness. The moral law would afterward speak in order to hold them within their proper limits and even to subject them all to a higher end which has no regard to inclination. But instead of the conflict which now the moral disposition has to wage with inclinations and in which, after some defeats, moral strength of mind may be gradually won, God and eternity in their awful majesty would stand unceasingly before our eyes (for that which we can completely prove is as certain as that which we can ascertain by sight). Transgression of the law would indeed be shunned, and the commanded would be performed. But because the disposition from which actions should be done cannot be instilled by any command, and because the spur to action would in this case be always present and external, reason would have no need to endeavor to gather its strength to resist the inclinations by a vivid idea of the dignity of the law. Thus most actions conforming to the law would be done from fear, few would be done from hope, none from duty. The moral worth of actions, on which alone the worth of the person and even of the world depends in the eyes of supreme wisdom, would not exist at all. The conduct of man, so long as his nature remained as it now is, would be changed into mere mechanism, where, as in a puppet show, everything would gesticulate well but no life would be found in the figures.

But it is quite otherwise with us. With all the exertion of our reason we have only a very obscure and ambiguous view into the future; the Governor of the world allows us only to conjecture His existence and majesty; not to behold or clearly prove them; the moral law in us, without promising or threatening us with anything certain, demands of us a disinterested respect; finally, only when this respect has become active and dominating, it allows us a view into the realm of the supersensible, though only a glimpse. Thus only can there be a truly moral character dedicated directly to the law and thus only can a rational creature become worthy of participating in the highest good corresponding to the moral worth of his person and not merely to his actions.

Thus what the study of nature and of man has suffi- [148] ciently shown elsewhere may well be true here, viz., that the inscrutable wisdom through which we exist is not less worthy of veneration in respect to what it denies us than in what it has granted.

PART II

METHODOLOGY OF PURE
PRACTICAL REASON

By the Methodology of pure practical reason we are [151] not to understand the manner of study or exposition which proceeds with pure practical principles for the purpose of a scientific knowledge of them, even though this procedure is the only one which is properly called "method" in theoretical reason. Popular knowledge requires a "manner," while science stands in need of a method, i.e., a procedure according to principles of reason, through which alone the manifold of knowledge can become a system. Here, on the contrary, we understand by methodology the way in which we can secure to the laws of pure practical reason access to the human mind and an influence on its maxims. That is to say, it is the way we can make objectively practical reason also subjectively practical.

Now it is clear that those motives of the will — the direct representation of the law and objective obedience to it as duty — which alone make the maxims really moral and give them a moral worth, must be thought of as the real drives of actions, for otherwise legality of actions but not morality of dispositions would result. But it is not so clear — in fact, it must appear highly improbable at first glance — that even subjectively the exhibition of pure virtue can have more power over the human mind, giving a far stronger drive to effectuate even that legality and to bring forward more powerful resolves to prefer the law to everything else merely out of respect for it, than all allurements arising from enjoyment and everything which may be counted as happiness or from all threats of pain and [152] harm. But it is really so, and if human nature were not so constituted, no way of presenting the law by circumlocutions and indirect recommendations could ever produce morality of dispositions. Everything would be mere cant; the law would be hated or even perhaps despised, though nevertheless followed for the sake of one's own advantage. The letter of the law (legality) would be met with in our actions, but the spirit of the law (morality) would not be found in our dispositions. Since with all our efforts we cannot completely free ourselves from reason in judging, we would inevitably appear to our own eyes as worthless and depraved men, even if we sought to compensate ourselves for this mortification before the inner tribunal by indulging in all the enjoyments which a supposed natural or divine law might be thought, in our delusion, to have connected with legality by means of a kind of police machinery regulating its operations by what we do without troubling itself about our motives for doing it.

Certainly it cannot be denied that in order to bring either an as yet uneducated or a degraded mind into the path of the morally good, some preparatory guidance is needed to attract it by a view to its own advantage or to frighten it by fear of harm. As soon as this machinery, these leading strings, have had some effect, the pure moral motive must be brought to mind. This is not only because it is the sole ground of character (a consistent practical habit of mind according to unchangeable maxims) but also because, in teaching a man to feel his own worth, it gives his mind a power, unexpected even by himself, to pull himself loose from all sensuous attachments (so far as they would fain dominate him) and, in the independence of his intelligible nature and in the greatness of soul to which he sees himself called, to find himself richly compensated for the sacrifice he makes. We should prove, by observations which anyone can make, that this property of our minds, this receptivity to a pure moral interest and the moving force in the pure thought of virtue when properly commended to the human heart, is the strongest drive to the good and indeed the only one when it is a question of continuous and meticulous obedience to [153] moral maxims. It must be remembered, however, that if these observations show only the reality of such a feeling but not any moral improvement resulting from it, this does no damage to the only method of making objectively practical laws of pure reason subjectively practical only through the pure thought of duty, nor does it pròve that this method is a vain phantasy. For since this method has never yet been widely used, experience can tell us nothing of its results; one can ask only for proofs of the receptivity to such drives which I shall briefly present and then in few words outline the method of founding and cultivating genuine moral dispositions.

If we attend to the course of conversation in mixed companies consisting not merely of scholars and subtle reasoners but also of business people or women, we notice that besides storytelling and jesting they have another entertainment, namely, arguing; for storytelling, if it is to have novelty and interest, soon exhausts itself, while jesting easily becomes insipid. Now of all arguments there are none which excite more ready participation by those who are otherwise soon bored with all subtle thinking, or which are more likely to bring a certain liveliness into the company, than one about the moral worth of this or that action from which the character of some person is to be made out. Those who otherwise find everything which is subtle and minute in theoretical questions dry and vexing soon take part when it is a question of the moral import of a good or bad act that is recounted; and they are exacting, meticulous, and subtle in excogitating everything which lessens or even casts suspicion on the purity of intention and thus on the degree of virtue to an extent we do not expect of them on any other subject of speculation. One can often see the character of the person who judges others revealed in his judgments. Some of them appear to be chiefly inclined, as they exercise their judicial office especially upon the dead, to defend the good that is related of this or that deed against all injurious charges of insincerity, finally protecting the entire moral worth of the person against the reproach of dissimulation and secret wickedness. Others, on the contrary, incline more to attacking this worth by accusations and fault-finding. But we cannot always ascribe to the latter the wish to argue away [154] virtue from all human examples in order to reduce it to an empty name; often it is a well-meaning strictness in the definition of genuine moral import according to an uncompromising law, in comparison with which (in contrast to comparison with examples) self-conceit in moral matters is very much reduced, and humility is not merely taught but is also felt by each in a penetrating self-examination. Nevertheless, we can often see, in the defenders of purity of intention in given examples, that where there is a presumption of righteousness they would gladly remove the least spot; and they do so lest, if all examples be disputed and all human virtue be denied its purity, virtue be held to be a mere phantom and all effort to attain it be deprecated as vain affectation and delusory conceit.

I do not know why the educators of youth have not long since made use of this propensity of reason to enter with pleasure upon the most subtle examination of practical questions put to the young, and why, after laying the foundation in a purely moral catechism, they have not searched through biographies of ancient and modern times with the purpose of having examples at hand of the duties they lay down, so that, by comparing similar actions under various circumstances, they could begin to exercise the moral judgment of their pupils in marking the greater or lesser moral significance of the actions. They would find that even very young people, who are not yet ready for speculation of other kinds, would soon become very acute and not a little interested, since they would feel the progress of their power of judgment; what is most important, they could confidently hope that frequent practice of knowing and approving of good conduct in all its purity, and of noting even the least deviation from it with sorrow or contempt, would leave a lasting impression of esteem for the one and disgust for the other, even though this practice is pursued only as a game of judgment in which children could compete with one another. By the mere habit of frequently looking upon actions as praiseworthy or blameworthy, a good foundation would be laid for righteousness in the future course of life. But I wish they [155] would spare them examples of so-called noble (super-meritorious) actions, which fill our sentimental writings, and would refer everything to duty only and the worth which a man can and must give himself in his own eyes through the consciousness of not having transgressed his duty, since whatever runs up into empty wishes and longings for unattainable perfection produces mere heroes of romance, who, while priding themselves on their feeling of transcendent greatness, release themselves from observing common and everyday responsibility as petty and insignificant.*

If one asks, however, what pure morality really is, by which, as the touchstone, the moral import of each action must be tested, I must confess that only philosophers can put the decision on this question in doubt. For by common sense it is long since decided, not by abstract general formulas but rather by habitual use, like the difference between the right and the left hand. We will therefore first show the distinctive mark of pure virtue in an example and, imagining that we have put it before, say, a ten-year-old boy for his judgment, see whether he must necessarily judge so by himself without being guided by the teacher.

Tell him the story of an honest man whom someone wishes to induce to join the calumniators of an innocent but powerless person (say, Anne Boleyn accused by Henry VIII of England). He is offered advantages, e.g., great gifts or high rank; he rejects them. This will cause only applause and approval in the [156] mind of the hearer, because they represent mere gain. Now

*It is entirely proper to extol actions which display a great, unselfish, and sympathetic disposition and humanity. But in them we must attend not so much to the elevation of soul, which is very fleeting and ephemeral, as to the subjection of the heart to duty, from which a more lasting impression can be expected as it entails principles and not just ebullitions, as the former does. One need only to reflect a little to find an indebtedness which the vaunted hero has in some way incurred to the human race (even if it be only that, by the inequality of men under the civil constitution, he enjoys advantages on account of which others must be lacking to just that extent), which will prevent the thought of duty from being repressed by the self-complacent imagination of merit.

come threats of loss. Among the slanderers there are his best friends who now renounce his friendship; near-relatives who threaten him (who is without fortune) with disinheritance; powerful persons who can persecute and harass him in all places and in every circumstance; a prince who threatens him with loss of freedom and even of life itself. But that the measure of his suffering may be full, so that he may feel the pain which only the morally good heart can very deeply feel, let his family, which is threatened with extreme need and want, entreat him to yield; think of the man himself, who, though righteous, has feelings which are not insensible or hardened to either sympathy or his own needs, at the moment when he wishes never to have lived to see the day which brings him such unutterable pain—think of him without any wavering or even a doubt remaining true to his resolution to be truthful—Thus one can lead the young listener step by step from mere approval to admiration, and from admiration to marveling, and finally to the greatest veneration and a lively wish that he himself could be such a man (though certainly not in his circumstances). Yet virtue is here worth so much only because it costs so much, not because it brings any advantage. All the admiration and even the endeavor to be like this character rest here solely on the purity of the moral principle, which can be clearly shown only by removing from the drive to the action everything which men might count as a part of happiness. Thus morality must have more power over the human heart the more purely it is presented. From this it follows that, if the law of morals and the image of holiness and virtue are to exert any influence at all on our minds, they can do so only in so far as they are laid to heart in their purity as drives unmixed with any view to welfare, because it is in suffering that they most notably show themselves. But a factor whose removal strengthens the effect of a moving force must have been a hindrance; consequently, all admixture of drives which derive from one's own happiness are a hindrance to the influence of the moral law on the human heart.

I assert further that, if in the admired action the motive from which it was done was esteem for duty, this respect for [157] the law, and not any pretension to inner greatness of mind or noble and meritorious sentiment, is that which has the most power over the mind of the spectator. Consequently, duty, not merit, has not only the most definite influence but, when seen in the true light of its inviolability, also the most penetrating influence on the mind.

In our times, when men hope to have more effect on the mind through yielding, soft-hearted feelings or high-flying, puffed-up pretensions, which wither instead of strengthening the heart, than through the dry and earnest idea of duty which is more fitting to human imperfection and progress in goodness, attention to this method is more needed than ever. One defeats his purpose by setting actions called noble, magnanimous, and meritorious as models for children with the notion of captivating them by infusing an enthusiasm for these actions. For as they are considerably backward in the observance of the commonest duty and even in the correct estimation of it, this amounts to speedily making them fantastic romancers. Even among the instructed and experienced portion of mankind, this supposed drive has, if not an injurious, at least no genuine moral, effect on the heart, which is what one hoped to produce by its means.

All feelings, and especially those which produce unusual exertions, must produce their effect in the moment when they are at their height and before they subside, else they have no effect at all. This is due to the fact that the heart naturally returns to its natural and moderate behavior and soon falls back into its previous languor because it has been brought into contact with something that stimulated it, not with something that strengthened it. Principles must be erected on concepts; on any other foundation there are only passing moods which give the person no moral worth and not even confidence in himself, without which the consciousness of his moral disposition and character, the highest good in man, cannot arise. These concepts, if they are to become subjectively practical, must not remain objective laws of morality which we merely admire and esteem in relation to mankind in general. Rather we must see the idea of them in relation to man as an individual, for then the law appears in a form which is indeed deserving of high [158] respect, though not as pleasing as if it belonged to the element to which he is naturally accustomed; on the contrary, it often compels him to leave this element, not without self-denial, and to give himself over to a higher element in which he can maintain himself only with effort and with unceasing apprehension of falling back into the former. In a word, the moral law demands obedience from duty, not from a predilection which cannot and should not be presupposed at all.

Let us now see in an example whether there is more subjective moving force of a drive in the thought of an action as noble and magnanimous than when the action is thought of merely as duty in relation to the solemn moral law. The action by which someone with the greatest danger to his own life seeks to save others in a shipwreck and at last loses his own life will indeed be counted, on the one hand, as duty, but on the other hand, even more as a meritorious action; but [in the latter case] our esteem for it will be weakened very much by the concept of his duty to himself, which here seems to have been infringed. More decisive is the magnanimous sacrifice of his life for the preservation of his country, and yet there still remain some scruples as to whether it is so perfect a duty to devote oneself spontaneously and unbidden to this purpose, and the action itself does not have the full force of a model and impulse to imitation. But if it is an inexorable duty, transgression against which violates of itself the moral law without respect to human welfare and, as it were, tramples on its holiness (the kind of duties which one usually calls duties to God, because we think of Him as the ideal of holiness in a substance), we give our most perfect esteem to pursuing it and sacrificing to it everything that ever had value for our dearest inclinations; and we find our soul strengthened and elevated by such an example when we convince ourselves, by contemplating it, that human nature is capable of such an elevation above everything that nature can present as a drive in opposition to it. Juvenal describes such an example in a climax which makes the reader vividly feel the power of the drive which lies in the pure law of duty as duty: "Be a stout soldier, a faithful guardian, and an incorrupt-ible judge; if summoned to bear witness in some dubious [159] and uncertain cause, though Phalaris himself should bring up his bull and dictate to you a perjury, count it the greatest of all sins to prefer life to honor, and to lose, for the sake of living, all that makes life worth living."[1]

Whenever we bring any flattering thought of merit into our actions, the drive is already mixed with self-love and thus has some assistance from the side of the sensuous. But to put every-thing else down below the holiness of duty and to know that we *can* do it because our own reason acknowledges it as its law and says that we *ought* to do it — that is, as it were, to lift our-selves altogether out of the world of sense; this elevation is in-separably present in the consciousness of the law as a drive of a faculty which rules over the sensuous, though not always effec-tively. But frequent concern with this drive and the at-first minor attempts at using it give hope of its effectiveness, so that gradually the greatest but still purely moral interest in it will be produced in us.

The method therefore takes the following course. The first step is to make judging according to moral laws a natural occu-pation which accompanies our own free actions as well as our observations of those of others, and to make it, as it were, a habit. We must sharpen these judgments by first asking whether the action is objectively in accordance with moral law, and if so, with which one; by this, heed to the law that gives only a *principle* of obligation is distinguished from one which is in fact obligatory (*leges obligandi a legibus obligantibus*).[2] For instance, we distinguish between the law of that which the

---

[1]Juvenal *Satire* viii. 79-84, trans. G. G. Ramsey ("Loeb Classical Library"). Phalaris was tyrant of Agrigentum who had a brass ox constructed in which his victims were burned to death.

[2]Laws of obligation [in general] distinguished from [specific] laws that [actu-ally] obligate.

needs of men require of me from that which their rights demand, the latter prescribing essential duties while the former prescribes nonessential duties. This teaches how to distinguish between the different duties which come together in an action.

The second point to which attention must be directed is the question as to whether the action is done (subjectively) for the sake of the moral law, and thus not only is morally correct as a deed, but also has moral worth as a disposition because of the maxim from which it was done. Now there is no doubt that this exercise and the consciousness of cultivation of our reason which judges concerning the practical must gradually produce a certain interest in its own law and thus in morally [160] good actions. For we ultimately take a liking to that the observation of which makes us feel that our powers of knowledge are extended, and this extension is especially furthered by that wherein we find moral correctness, since reason, with its faculty of determining according to a priori principles what ought to occur, can find satisfaction only in such an order of things. Even an observer of nature finally likes objects which first offend his senses when he discovers in them the great design of their organization, so that his reason finds nourishment in observing them; Leibniz spared an insect which he had carefully examined under the microscope, and replaced it on its leaf, because he had been instructed by viewing it and, as it were, had received a benefit from it.

But this occupation of the faculty of judgment, which makes us feel our own powers of knowledge, is not yet interest in actions and their morality itself. It only enables one to entertain himself with such judging and gives virtue or a turn of mind based on moral laws a form of beauty which is admired but not yet sought ("[Honesty] is praised and starves").[3] It is the same with everything whose contemplation produces subjectively a consciousness of the harmony of our powers of representation by which we feel our entire cognitive faculty (understanding and imagination) strengthened; it produces a satisfaction that

[3]*Laudatur et alget*, an allusion to Juvenal *Satire* i. 74.

can be communicated to others, but the existence of its object remains indifferent to us, as it is seen only as the occasion for our becoming aware of our store of talents which are elevated above the mere animal level.

Now the second exercise begins its work. It lies in calling to notice the purity of will by a vivid exhibition of the moral disposition in examples. It is presented first only as negative perfection, i.e., indicating that no drives of inclination are motives influencing an action done as a duty. By this, the pupil's attention is held to the consciousness of his freedom; and, although this renunciation [of the sensuous] excites an initial feeling of pain, at the same time, by relieving him of the constraint even of his true needs it frees him from the manifold discontent in which all these needs involve him and makes his mind receptive to the feeling of contentment from other sources. [161] The heart is freed from a burden which has secretly pressed upon it; it is lightened when in instances of pure moral resolutions there is revealed to man, who previously has not correctly known it, a faculty of inner freedom to release himself from the impetuous importunity of the inclinations, to such an extent that not even the dearest of them has an influence on a resolution for which he now makes use of his reason. In a case where I alone know that injustice lies in what I do, and where an open confession of it and an offer to make restitution is in direct conflict with vanity, selfishness, and an otherwise not illegitimate antipathy to the man whose rights I have impaired, if I can set aside all these considerations, there is consciousness of an independence from inclinations and circumstances and of the possibility of being sufficient to myself, which is salutary for me in yet other respects. The law of duty, through the positive worth which obedience to it makes us feel, finds easier access through the respect for ourselves in the consciousness of our freedom. If it is well established, so that a man fears nothing more than to find himself on self-examination to be worthless and contemptible in his own eyes, every good moral disposition can be grafted on to this self-respect, for the consciousness of freedom is the best, indeed the only, guard that can keep ignoble and corrupting influences from bursting in upon the mind.

With these remarks I have intended only to point out the most general maxims of the methodology of moral cultivation and exercise. Since the manifold variety of duties requires specific definitions of each kind, and these would constitute a prolix affair, the reader will excuse me if in a work like this, which is only preliminary, I go no further than these outlines.

CONCLUSION

Two things fill the mind with ever new and increasing wonder and awe, the oftener and the more steadily we reflect on them: the starry heavens above me and the moral law within me. I do not merely conjecture them and seek them as though obscured in darkness or in the transcendent region [162] beyond my horizon: I see them before me, and I associate them directly with the consciousness of my own existence. The heavens begin at the place I occupy in the external world of sense, and broaden the connection in which I stand into an unbounded magnitude of worlds beyond worlds and systems of systems and into the limitless times of their periodic motion, their beginning and their duration. The latter begins at my invisible self, my personality, and exhibits me in a world which has true infinity but which is comprehensible only to the understanding — a world with which I recognize myself as existing in a universal and necessary (and not, as in the first case, merely contingent) connection, and thereby also in connection with all those visible worlds. The former view of a countless multitude of worlds annihilates, as it were, my importance as an *animal creature*, which must give back to the planet (a mere speck in the universe) the matter from which it came, the matter which is for a little time provided with vital force, we know not how. The latter, on the contrary, infinitely raises my worth as that of an *intelligence* by my personality, in which the moral law reveals a life independent of all animality and even of the whole world of sense — at least so far as it may be inferred from the final destination assigned to my existence by this law, a destination which is not restricted to the conditions and boundaries of this life but reaches into the infinite.

But though wonder and respect can indeed excite to inquiry, they cannot supply the want of it. What, then, is to be done in order to set inquiry on foot in a useful way appropriate to the sublimity of its objects? Examples may serve for warnings here, but also for imitation. The observation of the world began from the noblest spectacle that was ever placed before the human senses and that our understanding can undertake to follow in its vast expanse, and it ended in — astrology. Morals began with the noblest attribute of human nature, the development and cultivation of which promised infinite utility, and it ended in — fanaticism or superstition. So it goes with all crude attempts in which the principal part of the business depends on the use of reason, a use which does not come of itself, like that of the feet, from frequent exercise, especially when it concerns attributes which cannot be so directly exhibited in common [163] experience. Though late, when the maxim did come into vogue of carefully examining every step which reason had to take and not to let it proceed except on the path of a well-considered method, the study of the structure of the world took an entirely different direction and therewith attained an incomparably happier result. The fall of a stone and the motion of a sling, resolved into their elements and the forces manifested in them treated mathematically, finally brought that clear and henceforth unchangeable insight into the structure of the world which, as observations continue, we may hope to broaden but need not fear having to retract.

This example recommends to us the same path in treating of the moral capacities of our nature and gives hope of a similarly good issue. We have at hand examples of the morally judging reason. We may analyze them into their elementary concepts, adopting, in default of mathematics, a process similar to that of chemistry, i.e., we may, in repeated experiments on common sense, separate the empirical from the rational, exhibit each of them in a pure state, and show what each by itself can accomplish. Thus we shall avoid the error of a crude and unpracticed judgment and (something far more important) the extravagances of genius, by which, as by the adepts of the philosopher's stone, visionary treasures are promised and real treasures are squandered for lack of methodical study and knowledge of nature. In a word, science (critically sought and methodically directed) is the narrow gate that leads to the doctrine of wisdom, when by this is understood not merely what one ought to do but what should serve as a guide to teachers in laying out plainly and well the path to wisdom which everyone should follow, and in keeping others from going astray. It is a science of which philosophy must always remain the guardian; and though the public takes no interest in its subtle investigations, it may very well take an interest in the doctrines which such considerations first make clear to it.